# The **ABC**'s of
# Who God Says I Am

# The **ABC**'s of
# Who God Says I Am

Kolleen Lucariello

TATE PUBLISHING
AND ENTERPRISES, LLC

Published by Tate Publishing & Enterprises, LLC
127 E. Trade Center Terrace | Mustang, Oklahoma 73064 USA
1.888.361.9473 | www.tatepublishing.com

Tate Publishing is committed to excellence in the publishing industry. The company reflects the philosophy established by the founders, based on Psalm 68:11,

*"The Lord gave the word and great was the company of those who published it."*

Book design copyright © 2013 by Tate Publishing, LLC. All rights reserved.
*Cover design by Rtor Maghuyop*
*Interior design by Jomar Ouano*

Published in the United States of America

ISBN: 978-1-62147-806-5
1. Religion / Christian Life / Devotional
2. Religion / Christian Life / General
12.12.13

# DEDICATION

It would be impossible for me to list each woman I hold dear to my heart, so for *all* of the beautiful woman in my life—my daughters and future granddaughters, my family and my sisters in Christ— I dedicate this book to each of you. My prayer is that each of you would look to Christ and the Word to discover who He says you are meant to be. I love each and every one of you.

# Acknowledgements

Throughout the years I have had many people come into my life for different seasons of growth. Some seasons have been short while others have stuck around for a very long time. One that has stayed with me is my incredible husband, Pat. He has been my greatest supporter. He has always encouraged me to try even when he knew I might need to fail. He is a man of grace and has showered it upon me continually. He has shown great patience as God began to change me and make me into the new creation He desired me to be. Pat, you are the most faithful, loving, and patient man I know. I love the memories that we have made together throughout the last thirty years, and I cannot wait to make thirty more years worth. I loved you in the eighth grade, and every day we share together I love you more. Thank you for showing me such unconditional love, allowing me to always be me, and for being my very best friend.

My beautiful children: Adam, Sarah, and Matt. You lived through the journey of change that the Lord took me on, and you survived. You have seen me at my ugliest, and yet you still call me a good mom. I adore you all and am blessed that God allowed me to be the one who was your momma. Jeffrey and Caroline, thank you for marrying into our family. I love that I can call you one of my kids. I am extremely thankful that God knew we needed you both in our family. I look forward to the years ahead of us as we grow together as family. I pray that you *all* allow the Lord to establish your steps and take you on the journey to become the person He designed you to be. Fulfill your purpose, please, and I pray you always remember who you really are. I love each of you. I also have a heart bursting full of gratitude to Caroline for helping me clear up my original draft of this book. Thank you for using your gifts and talents to help me clearly write what the Lord was putting on my heart. Oh—and I want to also say thank you for showing me the value of a Thesaurus.

Thank you, Kenda Beckwith, for your help, input and using your editing skills to frustrate and challenge me, (grin).

To my Bible study girls: Christine Garrett, you've stuck with me during the laughter and the tears, the highs and the lows, the clarity and the confusion. You have spoken truth to me that has corrected me and encouraged me, and most of all you have loved me just as I am. When others walked out of my life you remained a true and faithful friend. Thank you for being you and allowing me to be me. Cindy Shipley, thank you for the years of Bible study together. We have all grown and changed because of our time digging through God's Word for truth. You are an encouragement to many people, and I count myself blessed to be one of them. Sue Phillips and Kecia Schell, I had been given the vision for this book, and you were willing to walk through the rough draft of these pages with me. I loved our Thursday nights together and all that came out of them. Thank you for your comments, insights, and suggestions. You ladies bless me so much.

Jackie Ariola, Donnie always wanted to make a difference in people's lives. His death changed many people forever, myself included. I'm sorry we lost him for the remainder of our time here, but I think he would be so pumped to know that my relationship with the Lord grew out of his graduation from here to there, and I can't wait for the reunion.

Pastor Don and Diane Schell, who would have ever thought one day you would write the foreword for a book written by me? You two have always been such an important part of my life and a huge foundation in my faith. Your family is so very special to me, and I am blessed that the Lord allowed me to build so many of my memories around each member of the Schell family. I love you all so much.

There have been several Pastors whom, over the years, the Lord has had me sit under for teaching, training, rebuking and correcting. They have poured the Word into me. My relationship with God has become what it is because of my relationship with each of you. Proverbs 27:17 tells us that "as iron sharpens iron, so a friend sharpens a friend." I am so grateful for the sharpening in my life because of each one of you.

Thank you Tate Publishing for saying "yes" to my submission. This has been an unbelievable journey for me and a very special "thank you" to my Editor at Tate, Kathleen Dupré, for your help, advice and encouragement along the way.

Jesus, you died for me so I could live for you, and I am forever grateful. Thank you for saving me. I adore you.

# FOREWORD

Over the years Kolleen has played many different roles in our family. Being able to share some of those thoughts is a privilege. Since Diane's history is longer with Kolleen she will lead off.

Praise the Lord for the opportunity to share some of my life experiences with Kolleen. I have known her since she was very young when I babysat her and siblings. She has always been happy, inquisitive and fun to be around.

As a teenager Kolleen returned the favor and babysat our two older sons and our relationship drew closer during that time. She became a big part of our family and was the sister that I never had.

It has been exciting to see Kolleen over the years grow closer in her walk with the Lord. Her faith has grown and is she is open to being used by the Lord.

My relationship with Kolleen began after Diane and I married. Kolleen was a typical teen with the usual interests in things, sports, school, boys, especially one in particular. I think she was at our house every day, which was fine with us. I remember when we were painting our house and we came home to find Kolleen out there painting in our absence. Many evenings we would sit and watch TV together enjoying a bowl of ice cream, and when we got done Kolleen would say, "I think it's time for some popcorn."

After Pat and Kolleen married and moved away we lost a part of our lives, not just a babysitter. We would make every effort to get to see the Lucariellos and did not let the friendship die. The first time we let our oldest son spend the night away from home was with Pat and Kolleen. She became Aunt Kolleen to our children until they became adults. Our middle son, Ben, lived at the Lucariellos for months on two separate occasions.

Spiritually Kolleen continued to mature over the years. She became involved in the churches she attended. She reached out to anyone in need of help, especially youth. I know she played a big part in Ben's spiritual life while he was serving as Youth Pastor at her church in Parish.

We got to spend a week with Kolleen the summer of 2009 when we went to Kingdom Bound. It was a blessing to see the spiritually maturing Kolleen while not having lost the girl that could always make anyone laugh.

What Kolleen has written is not profound. The Lord has not used her to bring new knowledge to the Christian world. She was chosen to remind us of what we have read, heard and lived throughout our lives as Believers. You can take what she has given us with a grain of salt. But, remember what Jesus said in Matthew 5:13, "You are the salt of the earth. But if the salt loses its saltiness, how can it be made salty again? It is no longer good for anything, except to be thrown out and trampled by men."

Thank you, Kolleen, for spicing up our walk with the Lord.

—Pastor Don & Diane Schell
Millville United Methodist Church
Millville, DE

# INTRODUCTION

One day while I was reading a children's book to a special two-year-old on the *ABCs* I began to see different words other than what had been written for each letter. *A* no longer stood for apple, and *B* wasn't about a ball. The words that I began to see were words that I sensed the Lord using to describe me. Well, not only me, but you, too. He began to show me that He views us far differently than we view ourselves, and He took me on a journey. I am a pretty simple girl, and enjoy when the Lord makes things easy for me to understand. I think that is why He had me go through the alphabet. I discovered through the Word so much about who we really are. I learned that we are *a*ccepted no matter what we have done or where we've been. We are *b*eautiful to *b*ehold through the eyes of our Father. We have been *c*hanged—no longer the same as we once were. We are *d*esired by the God of the Universe. We have been *e*stablished, *f*orgiven and made *f*ree. We are God's children and because of that we are *h*oly and made in His *i*mage. We are *j*ustified from our sins. We are *k*nown and *l*oved. We have been given the *m*ind of Christ and have been made *n*ew, able to *o*vercome. God has given us a *p*urpose. We are *q*ualified by God to share in our inheritance. We are *r*ighteous and *s*ecure; nothing can separate us from Him. We are *t*reasured, *u*nderstood, and *v*ictorious, being full of *w*isdom, e*x*cluded from the world, and *y*oked to the King of Kings and Lord of Lords. I am ready and able to live a *z*ealous life in the fear of the Lord. Are you?

May you walk in the fullness of who God created you to be. Thank you for taking this journey with me through the *ABCs*. He made it quite clear to me that some things we are never too old to learn.

my parent's bathroom, open the medicine cabinet and take a syringe from the bottom shelf. My mother worked at the hospital and would, at times, forget to remove items from her pockets. I figured she wouldn't miss it and a couple of my friends and I had made a plan to use it to shoot alcohol into oranges to take on a school trip. At the time, I belonged to our school's touring chorus and we were leaving for an overnight stay in Canada to participate in a concert event. Before we left we had been given all the rules we were to follow and at the top of the list was zero tolerance for anyone who brought alcohol. A few of my fellow chorus members decided to see what they could get away with and when approached by them to participate, because I wanted desperately to fit in, I decided to go along with the plan. It worked. We were able to sneak oranges that were full of alcohol and small little bottles of alcohol onto the bus, and away we went. Now, my parents were very strict parents and I was not allowed to attend parties on the weekend, so I had never been drunk before. Little did I know at the time, but my friends had all conspired to get me drunk. They had their own little plan and it worked. Not only did I become drunk; I also became extremely sick. As in, all over the hotel room sick, and when I say all over, I mean *all* over. I still feel so bad for the hotel maid when I think of what she found the next morning— she had a terrible mess to clean up. The chorus had a very full day of singing and sightseeing planned for the next day and it was painful for me to endure. I did not imagine this trip with me having a pounding headache and queasy stomach. I had been looking forward to this time and now I could not even enjoy it. Not only had I broken the rules, but I had put myself in danger. The next day we were informed by our chaperones that other schools were in the hotel and there were several complaints about boys from other schools forcing themselves into the rooms of girls. When I staggered back to my room that night I had left the key in the door and made it possible for anyone to enter. I shudder now when I think about what could have happened to me, and am so thankful that it didn't.

What I have learned the hard way is this; the more I tried to win acceptance from others the more I needed to compromise what I knew was right in order to get it. I knew it was wrong to steal from my mother and I knew it was wrong to sneak alcohol on the bus; it was, in fact, illegal. I also knew it was wrong to spend the first night of our trip drinking. We were, after-all, underage, but I was too afraid of what my friends would think if I had said, "no." I wanted their approval and honestly, I wanted to finally feel like I fit in. It took some time for me to realize that when we live for the acceptance of man we risk becoming someone other than who the Creator has fashioned us to be. If you allow yourself to live for the acceptance of others for too long you will not know who you are or what you really believe. Your life becomes a lie. A struggle begins to stir within your mind and soul, and deep inside you know that no matter how hard you want acceptance you will not find it from people. That struggle between right and wrong is an overwhelming battle at times. There is a voice deep inside you longing to speak, and a message that needs to be heard, but fear of being unaccepted by others keeps you from sharing it. There are stands that need to be taken and challenges that should be made, but the fear of looking foolish keep us from taking and making them.

Fear of acceptance is not a new thing, nor is this a struggle I bear alone. We mold ourselves around society and have allowed ourselves to be intimidated by the status quo. We have sought the approval of men rather than God. We can find biblical evidence of this in John 12. Notice what it says at the beginning of verse forty-two.

> Nevertheless many even of the rulers believed in Him, but because of the Pharisees they were not confessing Him, for fear that they would be put out of the synagogue; for

they loved the approval of men rather than the approval of God (NASB).

John 12:42-43

There were leaders who believed that Jesus was Who He said He was, but because they loved the approval of man they would not confess Him. They allowed the fear of man to keep them from experiencing Jesus in all His fullness. It is a tragedy when fear prevents us from experiencing all that Jesus has for us.

What a tragedy it would have been had Mary allowed the opinion of others to keep her from experiencing an intimate moment she shared with Jesus. Mary anointed Jesus's feet with expensive perfume, and the disciples did not accept it, yet Jesus accepted it. In fact, He defended her. We find her story in John 12:1-8.

> Then, six days before the Passover, Jesus came to Bethany, where Lazarus was who had been dead, whom He had raised from the dead. There they made Him a supper; and Martha served, but Lazarus was one of those who sat at the table with Him. Then Mary took a pound of very costly oil of spikenard, anointed the feet of Jesus, and wiped His feet with her hair. And the house was filled with the fragrance of the oil. But one of His disciples, Judas Iscariot, Simon's son, who would betray Him, said, "Why was this fragrant oil not sold for three hundred denarii and given to the poor?" This he said, not that he cared for the poor, but because he was a thief, and had the moneybox; and he used to take what was put in it. But Jesus said, "Let her alone; she has kept this for the day of My burial. For the poor you have with you always, but Me you do not have always.

John 12:1-8

The disciples couldn't understand the significance of this act, but Jesus did. He knew the spiritual significance behind it. Have you ever known something to be true in your heart but would not allow yourself to speak it for fear of what others around you would think and say? Especially when it comes to our faith, we have an overwhelming fear that we are going to look or sound foolish if we speak up for what we believe in. The truth is there is a good chance that you *will* be looked at foolishly. We can read that in 1 Corinthians 1:18. "For the message of the cross is foolishness to those who are perishing, but to us who are being saved it is the power of God." With today's view that everything and anything goes, a Christ-centered view is not widely and openly received—even among Christians. Speaking about what God is doing in your life or a revelation He has given you from His Word might not sit well, especially if it brings conviction to others. For example, Judas sat with Jesus, and rather than worship at His feet, as Mary was doing, he rebuked her for being wasteful! Oh, that we would consider the worship of another's heart before we begin our rebukes!

In my humble opinion, acceptance means a place where I can go and be my *true* self and know that I will be shown the grace, love, and mercy we all long for. I will never have to fear being cut off because I did not adhere to the standards of society. This does not mean that everything I say or do is right and I should never be confronted. Acceptance means that no matter what mistakes I make, or how mad I make others, they will still accept me for who I am and love me just the same. Sounds a little unconditional, doesn't it? Well, that is what Christ's acceptance brings to me. And that is what He gave to the woman caught in the act of adultery as told to us by John.

> Now early in the morning He came again into the temple, and all the people came to Him; and He sat down and taught them. Then the scribes and Pharisees brought to

...my heart swells. It is humbling for me to think that He has blessed me with every spiritual blessing and chose me before the foundation of the world. He also knew He would call me His own, and He provided a way for me to be accepted by Him. God has accepted me. Just as I am, He has accepted me. When I offered my heart to Him He received me "especially with gladness and approval."

In the Greek translation, the word accepted is *charitoo*, which means "highly favored." In a world where there is very little acceptance of one another, God wants us to know and understand that we are accepted by Him. I am highly favored. You are highly favored. At this point in my life I have finally found the acceptance I have been longing for, and I will never tamper with an orange again. The God of the universe has accepted me as His own; what more could I ask for? What more could *you* ask for?

Questions to consider:

1)  What does acceptance look like to you?

2)  Have you ever compromised yourself or done something that you knew was wrong for the acceptance of others?

3)  What do some people do for acceptance?

4)  What does God say in Psalm 56:9? Is He for us or against us?

5)  Why do you think we allow ourselves to be controlled by the need for others acceptance?

6)  Have you ever had a hard time accepting someone?

7) How can you come to a place in your mind where you completely trust the fact that God accepts you? What steps will you take to believe this truth?

8) How can we separate our, or others, unacceptable behavior while not forgetting we are still acceptable to God?

9) Read John 12 and list all of the ways people looked for acceptance. Whose acceptance were they looking for?

# B Is for Beautiful

## "God Says I am *Beautiful*"

"All *beautiful* you are, my darling; there is no flaw in you."

Song of Solomon 4:7

*Beauty*: the quality present in a thing or person that gives intense pleasure or deep satisfaction to the mind, whether arising from sensory manifestations (as shape, color, sound, etc.), a meaningful design or pattern, or something else (as a personality in which high spiritual qualities are manifest) (dictionary.com, LLC, 2011).

One day I was watching television and saw a commercial for Dove Soap. The commercial was about a campaign for beauty. They had different young girls share their definition of beauty. My curiosity was piqued, so after checking out their website, I found out that Dove developed an advertising campaign about true beauty based on the opinion of a range of women. The goal was to spark a national discussion in widening the definition of beauty. Dove's website includes statistics that state, "Only 2 percent of women around the world: describe themselves as beautiful... 81 percent of US women strongly agree that the media and advertising set an unrealistic standard of beauty that most women could not ever achieve" (Dove, 2011).

They have some great videos on learning to love yourself just as you are. It is a noble message, but I believe they are leaving out a very important aspect of beauty. How can we ever stop obsessing over physical flaws and begin to be comfortable with how we look if we leave out the *spiritual* aspect? I truly believe it is God, through His Word, who can really teach us and show us what real beauty is. Isn't it intriguing that one of the definitions of beauty is "a personality in which high spiritual qualities are manifest?"

When I was younger my appearance was very important to me, and I admit that I thought about how I looked a lot. One area where I was very insecure with was my teeth. I had a gap between my two front teeth. When I looked in the mirror, all I saw was a very large gap, and I allowed it to torment me. It did not help that I also had an older brother who loved to pick on me about this, so my insecurity was tremendous. I never liked to smile because I believed that when I did all people could see was the gap between those teeth. I begged for braces, and when the dentist told me I did not need them, I cried. I wondered how he could say that, but all he would tell me was to be patient and that they would grow together. That did not help me. I wanted them fixed now, so I decided to take matters into my own hands. I subjected my mouth to a range of torture devices ranging from rubber bands to the metal backs of barrettes, which I would pinch tightly onto my teeth—anything I thought might help my teeth grow together. Oh, this gives me a chuckle now, thinking of how silly I must have looked. Here I wanted to look good, but I was willing to do things that made me look ridiculous for it! I wanted to look good on the outside, to make an impression on others with my looks, but rarely did I give thought to how I looked on the inside. When I look back I must confess that I was rather ugly at times, not because of my outward appearance so much (although there were times there was truth to that as well!) but because when I opened my mouth it wasn't my teeth that made me so ugly; it was the ugliness coming out of me. I could be loud and demanding and honestly there were times when I was downright mean. We were a church-going family, so at home, I was pretty careful with my words, but once I got to school I was not the least bit careful. I could be extremely foul-mouthed. I am really quite embarrassed when I remember the language that I allowed to come forth from my lips. I did not want to appear to be the "Good Girl" just because I was a "Church Girl," so my mouth was my tool of choice. I used it to prove I could cuss like the rest of them. I do remember my mother picking me up from sporting practice at the school one night and forgetting with whom I was sitting next to and I let a curse word slip through the doorway of my mouth. Believe me, my mother was not impressed. I also knew I had better never speak like that around her again. In fact, I knew that it was wrong for me to speak like that at all. Now, when I reminisce on those days I wonder why I thought there was anything attractive or appealing about using language that was really quite rude. It also became a hard habit to break. I also began to stuff a lot of anger inside of me which, when released, was a very unattractive sight for anyone to behold. My temper tantrums were dangerous for anyone to witness as words were used that would cut to the core, along with a few items flying here and there. If I wasn't throwing a temper tantrum I was pouting. I can see now that I spent many years of my life mad and angry about something.

We are mistaken when we believe that beauty has everything to do with our physical appearance, and we are missing God when that becomes our focus. Here's why; Proverbs 11:22 says, "Like a gold ring in a pig's snout is a beautiful woman who shows no discretion." It would be silly to put a gold ring in a pig's snout, and that's the point of the verse; it is silly for a beautiful woman to not have discretion. It takes away from your beauty.

As I get older and the arms aren't quite as firm or more wrinkles appear and the body is not quite in the shape it once was, I have to be careful where I allow my focus to go. I could become completely consumed by how I *used* to look or what size I *used* to wear. I have heard women my age talk about the attention that they *used* to be able to get from men. The heads they *used* to be able to turn. We all have seen the shows and heard about the great lengths that women go to just to remain beautiful in the eyes of the world. Why do we do that? We cannot possibly keep up with standards because the world's measure of beauty is always changing. But the Word says that, "Charm is deceitful and beauty is passing, but a woman who fears the Lord, she shall be praised" (Proverbs 31:30). If beauty is passing then we must come to the place in our heart where we say, "God, I want to be beautiful from the inside out and beautiful for you." More than anything in my life, at this point in my walk with the Lord, I want to know what He considers beautiful. I want to be beautiful to Jesus. I know that if I am beautiful to Him I will be beautiful to others. So we must look at the Word to discover what God says real beauty is all about.

Several years ago a friend of mine, who worked at a local bank, told me something about our daughter that I have never forgotten. Our daughter loves the Lord, and she has always had a tender heart for Him. One day she went into the bank to make a deposit. After she left, the teller who waited on her said this to my friend: "That Sarah, she is beautiful inside and out, and she doesn't even know it." I was so blessed by that statement. What that woman saw in her was the Spirit of God living in her, and her beauty came from within.

> Don't be concerned about the outward beauty of fancy hairstyles, expensive jewelry, or beautiful clothes. You should clothe yourselves instead with the beauty that comes from within, the unfading beauty of a gentle and quiet spirit, which is so precious to God.
>
> 1 Peter 3:3-4

Beauty that comes from a gentle, quiet spirit is precious to God. Is a gentle, quiet spirit precious to the world? Not always, but should we live for the world or for God? By the world's standards or God's?

A few years ago there was a television show called *True Beauty* that my husband and I caught every now and then. In this show contestants were competing for the grand prize of $100,000 and to be featured in *People Magazine*'s "100 Most Beautiful People" issue. What they did not realize is that while the people on the show thought they were being judged on physicality, they actually were being judged on their inward beauty. The cameras were rolling as the contestants were put in many different scenarios and then judged by how well they responded to the situation. Sometimes, while they may have *looked* beautiful on the outside, what came out from the inside was just downright ugly. Temper tantrums and poor attitudes ruled the house they lived in. While most only looked out for themselves and what they wanted, in the end there would be only one that exhibited true beauty from the inside out. We can work all day long on making ourselves look impressive to others, but it is important to remember that God's camera is always rolling, and He is always judging us by our inward heart.

As I get older I am sure that there will be times when I look in the mirror and probably wince at what I see (even more so than I do now!), but when my mind wants to begin to pick apart all of the physical flaws, it is then that I want to turn my focus on what the Lord sees. I want to hear, "You are altogether beautiful, my darling; there is no flaw in you." (Song of Solomon 4:7). I love the fact that Dove is choosing natural, everyday women to represent them, but I refuse to allow the beauty industry to set my standard for what defines beauty. Rather, I choose to allow God to set those standards for me. Let's get alone before Him and ask Him to help us radiate the beauty of a gentle, quiet spirit before a world that knows anything but. In the Dove commercial

I viewed, the little girl said, "I will remind myself every day that I am beautiful." That is a good rule to live by. I would only add, "I will remind myself every day that *God* says I am beautiful."

Questions to consider:

1) How would you define true beauty?

2) Do you struggle with your looks? If you do, where is your struggle? What can you do to begin to turn this over to the Lord?

3) What is the difference in someone who is beautiful on the outside verses someone who is beautiful on the inside?

4) Have you ever known someone to be beautiful on the outside yet ugly on the inside?

5) Read Esther 1. Why did the King want Vashti to come? Was there any beauty in her response?

6) What do you think it means to "fear the Lord"?

7) Do you understand what a healthy fear of the Lord is? Would you say you have a healthy fear of the Lord?

8) Read Psalm 27:4. What is it we should seek after and why?

9) What steps can we take to block out the worlds standard of beauty and live in God's standard?

# C Is for Changed

## "God Says I am *Changed*"

"The Spirit of the LORD will come upon you in power, and you will prophesy with them; and you will be *changed* into a different person."

1 Samuel 10:6

*Change*: to become different, to transform or convert (dictionary. com, 2011).

When I first accepted the fact that God could do a better job running my life than I could, I know that I did not give much thought about the changes He would make in me. I knew that I needed *a* change, but it did not occur to me then that the truth was; I needed *to* change. The truth is we all have a tendency to believe that everything that happens to us is because of some other person or situation. I am no different. It was easy for me to blame my unhappiness on everyone else. But there were things about me, some perceptions, attitudes, deep wounds, and, let's say, personality traits, that God knew needed to be changed. And since He was the One capable of making the changes, change He did. But I had to allow Him access to my heart to do His work and begin construction on the areas He desired to change. I also had to allow the people He saw fit to bring into my life and use in the process of change to do what He wanted them to do. I believe that people are brought into our lives for a "God-purpose," and it is important to allow them to sharpen us. Proverbs 27:17 says, "As iron sharpens iron, so one man sharpens another." As people move in and out of our lives, we can ask God what His purpose is for this relationship. What change does God intend to bring to my life through them?

The Lord gave me a dream one night many years ago shortly after I sincerely surrendered my heart to Him. It was one of those dreams that's just so real to ever forget. I was sitting at a picnic table with friends and family when I felt as though I was going to be very sick. I also began to feel what felt like a string in my mouth.

So with my right hand I reached up, and when I pulled on the string a boot emerged. You read correctly—a *boot*! After a few minutes I felt the same sensation, and I pulled the string again; this time a tin can emerged. This went on for some time, and I pulled out a tire, more tin cans, and many miscellaneous junk items. At that point in my life the Lord had placed a strong Christian mentor in my life; I called her up and told her about my disturbing dream. After a brief silence her response to me was, "It sounds to me like you have a lot of junk inside of you, and God wants to pull it out." Instantly I knew she was right. I experienced a sense of peace that her words were correct, and I had a choice to make. I could shut my mouth and refuse to allow God access to all that was inside of me. I could give Him access to certain areas of my life and keep others off limits to Him, or I could let Him have *all* of me. Every part of my heart could belong to Him, and I could give Him permission to change me. I had no choice; the only option for me was to surrender my heart to Him and let Him change me. I asked Him to make me the person He wanted me to be. I wanted to change completely, and I realized that the change was going to start from the inside and work its way out. Once I began to surrender to the Lord, He, in turn, began to reveal His Word to me. I would read the Word or hear it spoken in church and He would begin to show me where I was out of step with Him, how I was behaving in a way that was not pleasing to Him or where I misunderstood His Word. He used a Pastor speaking on Ephesians 4:26 to show me that in my anger I *was* in sin and that needed to change. The Lord began to show me that I used my anger to control others and that I needed to allow Him to help me stop allowing my anger to control *me*. One Sunday while sitting in church listening to our Pastor's message I felt certain that it was for my friend, sitting next to me, and I told God all about it. "Lord, this is so great for him to hear. He really needed to hear this now." As I allowed my mind to consider it the Pastor said: "Now don't think that this is for the person sitting next to you. God is speaking to *you*." I could not believe I had just heard him say that and with that comment came a new revelation- pride. God showed me that day that I was not supposed to go to church and decide that the message was for someone else. I needed to always apply it to my own life. I always needed to assume that God was speaking to *me*, placing His truth directly into *my* heart, for *me*, not for my neighbor, or my husband, or my children. God wanted *me* to listen to His Word so He could make me into the person He designed me to be; that was not going to happen if I sat stoic in my seat always believing the message did not apply to *me*. That it was somehow irrelevant to *my* life. I began to listen intently, asking the Lord to reveal His truth to me—my hope was to walk out of every church service or every Bible study transformed. God was beginning to pull the garbage out of the area that held so much junk that it hurt. My heart.

That's where God begins—with the heart. He tells us through His Word what He wants to do with our heart. "I will give you a new heart and put a new spirit in you; I will remove from you your heart of stone and give you a heart of flesh" (Ezekiel 36:26). My cold, bitter, old heart that once held so much bitterness, anger, and resentment—God took it. In its place He put a heart filled with compassion, love, and a desire for all God has for me. He helped me see life from a different perspective—His.

In Ephesians 4, Paul tells us to let go of our old man and put on a new man. The old is full of deceit.

> But you have not so learned Christ, if indeed you have heard Him and have been taught by Him, as the truth is in Jesus: that you put off, concerning your former conduct, the old man which grows corrupt according to the deceitful lusts, and be renewed in the spirit of your mind, and that you put on the new man which was created according to God, in true righteousness and holiness.
>
> Ephesians 4:20-23

We must get our minds wrapped around the fact that the old is gone and the new has come. It is not just mere words in a book. It is truth for us to hold on to. The verse from 1 Samuel 10:6 was spoken to Saul after Samuel had anointed him commander of the Lord's inheritance (1 Samuel 10:1). He was going to be King over Israel, but Saul did not see himself as a king. Instead he responded, "Am I not a Benjamite, of the smallest of the tribes of Israel, and my family the least of all the families of the tribe of Benjamin? Why then do you speak like this to me?" (1 Samuel 9:21). Saul did not see himself as a king; he saw himself as "small" and "least." But that's not how God saw him. He was the man God had chosen for the Israelites' king. It takes faith on our part to view ourselves as God does. That's also true in how we view the potential of others. When other people, or myself for that matter, try convincing me that I will never change, I must remind myself that change does not happen overnight. I can continue to change for the rest of my life here on earth. I cannot stand to hear people say of others, "They'll never change," because I know

4) What area in your life do you see that God has changed the most?

5) Different translations use the phrase "turned into another man" in 1 Samuel 10:6 rather than *changed*. Do you believe God has the ability to change a person so drastically that they can become a completely different person?

6) Have you fully surrendered your whole heart to the Lord, allowing Him to change you, transform you, and turn you into the person He has called you to be?

7) If not, why? What do you think keeps you from fully surrendering your heart to Him?

8) Read Psalm 139:23-24. What can we ask God to do within us?

9) What can we learn from Psalm 141:5 about the value of accountability?

# D IS FOR DESIRE

## God Says He *Desires* Me

"So will the King *desire* your beauty; because He is your Lord, be submissive and reverence and honor Him."

Psalm 45:11

*Desire:* a longing or craving, as for something that brings satisfaction or enjoyment (dictionary.com, 2011).

I am not sure if you were like me as a child, but when I was a little girl I used to dream about my wedding day. Each week one of my best friends and I would look through the bridal section in the Sunday newspaper. I laugh as I think back on it, remembering how we would sit for the longest time and look at all the pictures of the brides and choose which one we were going to look like when we were old enough to get married. It was fun to daydream as a little girl about the beautiful dress and the wedding that I would have when I was old enough. Every girl wants to feel like a princess, don't they? Of course they do! That's why the world was so captivated by the royal wedding of Prince William and Catherine, Duchess of Cambridge. We all love a fairy tale, and I was no different. As I grew into a young woman the daydreams began to give way to a desire. I began to have a deep desire for that certain someone who would bring satisfaction and enjoyment to my life. I wanted a fairy tale wedding to my Prince Charming.

My personal fairy tale began when I became engaged to a wonderful man. He was my high school sweetheart and the man I loved more than anything. After years of preparation and planning I finally became a real bride. (I wonder if a little girl cut my picture out from the paper?) Even though my wedding was several decades ago, I remember the feelings I experienced as a bride very clearly. My heart held anticipation and excitement for our future together. We had spent many hours together through the years, getting to know one another and learning to trust and understand each other. We met at the altar as two individuals and walked out of the church united together as one. My wedding day was one of the happiest days of my life. I know that I felt like a princess that day and that God had brought me my prince. Our wedding was not quite as elaborate as the royal wedding; we gathered at a small church in Western New York and held a reception at the local fire hall. But the love of family and friends surrounded us and we were excited to walk out the doors of that fire hall and into our future.

As I watched the news coverage on the royal wedding I was reminded again of my wedding day and the joy of being a bride. But I also began to think about another royal wedding that will someday be upon us. We have been given a promise in the scriptures of the wedding of the Bridegroom, Jesus, with His radiant bride, His church. One day Jesus is coming back for His Bride, the Bride of Christ, which is the church; those who have accepted His gift of salvation. Similar to the dreams of my own wedding as a girl, we as Christians can now look forward to the day when Jesus returns and gathers His bride. As we hold desire in our hearts of the day we will marry our Bridegroom, God has desire for us and He wants us to prepare for that day.

The relationship between a bride and groom is incredibly intimate and is made physically tangible on the wedding day.

Isaiah 62:5b says, "And as the bridegroom rejoices over the bride, so shall your God rejoice over you." When I am at a wedding one of my favorite moments is when the bride enters and the groom views her for the first time. I quickly look at her, but then I look at him and watch his reaction to her entrance. There is a depth of emotion in his eyes, which I dare say one would have a hard time putting into words. I watched our own children look into the eyes of their future spouses on their wedding days, and I could see the joy, the anticipation, and the desire within them. When they stood and pledged their love to one another they made a promise of commitment. The intimate looks they gave one another all through the day spoke quietly and softly the unspoken words of love for one another. As our son took his bride and our son-in-law took his, there was visible rejoicing over their new brides. Their love runs deep for one another, and in the same way our Heavenly Father's love runs deep, and He, too, rejoices over us and has desire for us. Take a moment and consider how lovingly He must look upon us. How tender He is and how precious we are to Him. Psalm 139:17 says, "How precious also are your thoughts to me, O God! How great is the sum of them!" The Hebrew word for precious, *Yaqar*, means; "to esteem, be prized, be valuable, be precious, be costly, and be appraised" (Strong's 3365). I am a prize to God; you are a prize to God. We are His bride, and He is looking for us to be without "spot or wrinkle or any such thing, but that she should be holy and without blemish" (Ephesians 5:27), preparing ourselves for His return.

I will be honest and tell you that there have been times I was not able to view myself as much of a prize. Certainly not a valuable, precious prize. I'm really not all that desirable some days; in fact, there are moments when I can be just plain ugly. When I allow myself to be controlled by my feelings, my actions can sometimes be pretty undesirable. Oh how I despise that ugly side of me. Miraculously, I have married a man with the gift of grace. He has loved me on my good days and through all my bad days. I see the Spirit of God in him because I know that somehow God, too, looks past the ugliness and still sees the desirable me.

Not only does God desire a relationship with me, but He also wants an intimate relationship. When I first became a Christian and heard messages that suggested I become intimate with the Lord, I wondered how that was possible. Looking back now on thirty years of marriage, my relationship with my husband has become even more intimate as we continue to grow closer. We have endured both good and bad times together and now experience a deeper level of commitment than on our wedding day. My desire is for my husband alone. I would never want to hurt him in any way. In fact, I love to be a blessing to him. If someone had told me on my wedding day that the love I had for him at that moment would be the least amount I would have, I would never have believed it. But it is true. Every day I spend with him my love grows deeper. And just as the love for my husband has grown through the years, so has my love for the Lord. As I have spent time in His Word, learning about Him and getting to know Him, I have developed a deeper understanding and a much more intimate relationship with Him. The beauty for me is that God desires that relationship.

For some of us it can be hard to believe that God would find us desirable and want to be intimate with us. In our minds we replay the things we've done or maybe were done to us that we view as so damaging and dirty it is almost impossible to view ourselves as the pure and spotless bride Jesus is coming back for. But, my friend, that is the beauty of the cross that Jesus suffered and died for us on. David cried out to God in Psalm 51 after his sin with Bathsheba was revealed. He said, "Purify me with hyssop, and I shall be clean: Wash me, and I shall be whiter than snow" (Psalm 51:7). I love the way the Message Bible states the same verse. "Soak me in your laundry and I'll come out clean, scrub me and I'll have a snow-white life" (Psalm 51:7). Oh, God is so good to us. He desires us to hold back nothing from Him. He desires our time, our love, our devotion, our hearts, our thoughts, and our dreams. Just like a new bride and her bridegroom spend countless hours getting to know one another in a more intimate way, Christ, our Bridegroom, desires the same. Won't you pray right now and ask God to help you become the pure, spotless bride He is coming back for?

Questions to consider:

1) What does a bride do to prepare for her wedding day?

2) Read Matthew 25:1-13. Explain what Jesus is talking about in this parable.

3) What must we do as the Bride of Christ to prepare for His return?

4) Is it easy or hard for you to believe you are desired by God?

5) Do you have an intimate relationship with God, or would you say it is more casual?

6) Issues from the past can keep us from believing God would want an intimate relationship with us. Do you know of any that might hinder this level of relationship for you? If so, can you believe that God wants to wash you and make you whiter than snow?

7) Pray and ask God to take you deeper in your relationship. Give Him permission to move in your life, to take you as deep as *He* wants to go.

# E IS FOR ESTABLISHED

## God Says He Has *Established* My Steps

I waited patiently for the Lord; and He inclined to me, and heard my cry. He also brought me up out of a horrible pit, Out of the miry clay, and set my feet upon a rock, and *established* my steps. He has put a new song in my mouth–Praise to our God; Many will see it and fear, and will trust in the Lord.

Psalm 40:1-3

*Establish*: 1. to place or settle in a secure position or condition; install. 2. To make firm or secure (dictionary.com, 2011).

I have a confession to make. I am not a patient person. Not patient at all. I would love to say that you could look up the word *patient* in the dictionary and see my name next to it, but that would not happen. Due to my lack of patience, I have set out on many journeys to fulfill my purpose, only to discover that my steps were either out of God's timing or completely out of His will. I can now see that every time I stepped ahead of God I was striving, in my own strength, to make His will happen for my life. I desperately wanted to be in His will, and I had a sense of what that looked like. The wait was just taking too long for my liking. So once I had an idea or a thought of what God might have for me, *zoom!* I was off and running, always leaving God behind. Unfortunately for me, when I stepped out before God and tried to move the mountains on my own, once the dream collapsed and failure followed, so did the three Ds: disappointment, discouragement, and depression. Thankfully the Lord is patient where I am not, and I can now see that all the roads I traveled brought me to a place where I could read Psalm 40 and offer it as my own personal prayer. Through the hard times of striving and waiting, I can now see clearly that God is always in the waiting.

One day I decided that I needed to pick apart the first three verses of Psalm 40. What a great lesson the Lord taught me that day. The Hebrew translation for "I waited patiently" is literally "waiting I waited." "Waiting…I waited," I just couldn't get over that. I absolutely love David's heart; there is so much we can learn from him. I am not sure what trouble he was going through at the time he wrote this Psalm, but I know that he was a man who understood trouble. He walked through plenty of hard times. Through each trial he faced he always found that he needed to rely solely on God for all his needs. David was a man that God called "a man after His own heart" (Acts 13:22). Yet he still was a man, a human just like you and me, who fell into troubled times during his life. Each and every time David cried out for the Lord, He was there to meet him. In the first verse of Psalm 40, David wrote the Lord, "inclined to him," which reminded me of a parent running towards their children when a child is crying out for help. Most parents move pretty quickly when they hear their own child's unmistakable cry for help. And like a child who is waiting to be rescued, David tells us that while he was waiting for God to move, he just waited. Patiently he waited and the Lord heard his cry, and He bent down toward him and lifted him out of the abominable pit he was in. David might have written this Psalm when he found himself running from Saul, hiding in caves and wondering how and when God was going to get him out of his present situation. God had anointed David to be king, and yet he found himself hiding from the current king who wanted to kill him. How did he make the transition from shepherd boy to future king and then from killing Goliath to a man on the run? Those were some of the circumstances that contributed to David seeking after God. It was during his time in this pit that drew him closer to the Lord. And if we keep our eyes focused on God, our time in the pit can draw us closer, as well.

But if you are anything like me, being stuck in the mire is not all that appealing. Oh, I have been there a time or two. I may not have been physically stuck in the mud—well, truth be told, once or twice I actually *have* gotten stuck in some mud, but that's not the kind of mud we are talking about. At times I have felt suffocated by the horrible pit, surrounded by so much miry clay. I really thought I would die there. Many times throughout the years I believed God would answer my prayers a certain way, and when the answer was different I was crushed. Then I would allow my two friends, Hurt and Disappointment, to take me by the hand and lead me right into the miry clay. Once I was there, climbing back out seemed too great a feat to overcome. In fact, I once had a minister praying for me say, "Hope deferred makes the heart sick." That was a perfect description of me—heartsick over every deferred hope. At the time he spoke those words to me I was trying to make my will be God's will. I was hoping that God would say yes to what I wanted rather than me saying yes to what He wanted. I was extremely selfish and everything needed to happen on my terms. In fact, my husband nicknamed me "Mrs. Oneway." Then, when my hopes fell apart, so would I. I was like a two-year-old girl having a temper tantrum. Have you ever felt as though perhaps physically you weren't walking in "mire," but you were going through something that made you feel as though you might as well be? Every step can feel heavy and defeated and completely unbearable. I believe most of us have experienced the metaphysical *pit* at one time or another. But that should never be our dwelling place. How do we escape?

After the Lord bent toward David, He reached down and lifted David out of the pit of destruction and He set his feet on a rock and established his steps. When I read this, I just have to stop and spend a few moments giving thanks. What a promise of hope! Just like in the classic films, I can visualize the hero rescuing the damsel in distress. God will reach down and put me on a rock. Interestingly enough, one of the Hebrew translations of rock is '...stronghold of Jehovah, of security" (Strong's H5553), which, I believe, is an accurate description of God.

God is referred to as a "Rock" in the scriptures. He wants to reach down and pull me out of the pit I am in and set me upon Himself, upon the Rock of His Word, upon the Rock of His foundation and truth. Then David says that the Lord "steadied my steps and established my goings" (Psalm 40:2). In Hebrew the word established has several different definitions. Some of these are "to be firm, be stable, to be fixed, be securely determined, be secure, be enduring, to be directed aright, be fixed aright, be steadfast (in a moral sense)" (Strongs, Blue Letter Bible, 1996-2011). Once I realized that the Word was the ladder that would help me climb out of the pit and walk securely determined and steadfast, I began to devour each word.

The truth is we all have spent time in miscellaneous pits. The pit that leads to destruction can look like the pit of depression, or it might be a pit of fear and insecurity. There are pits full of alcoholism and drug abuse, the pit of pornography, or the pit of discouragement and despair. There are pits of low self-esteem and the pit of past regrets. The pits of jealousy and envy aren't much fun. I have spent my share of time in each of those pits. Years ago I was hurt by a good friend, and because of the hurt I began to grow more and more critical of her. She could do nothing right in my eyes. I did not realize that what I thought was a hurt on her part was actually jealousy on mine. The Lord revealed the truth of my own heart when I read this verse, "Anger is cruel and fury overwhelming, but who can stand before jealousy" (Proverbs a very high paying job, too, but eventually I realized I was the one paying. It was costing me a great deal, and I did not reap any benefits from it other than a bitter, resentful, hateful heart and broken relationships. I was not very fun to be around. I am extremely grateful now that I no longer have to be that person.

Sometimes I struggled with wrongs done against me. Other times the sins of my past would torment me on a daily basis. Offering forgiveness to ourselves and others may prove worse than physical torture, but living in perpetual blame is ultimately worse; it is like a torture device. We just cannot forgive because, after all, we feel it is within our rights to hold onto that grudge. How easily we forget just how much we have been forgiven. We enjoy keeping mental records of wrongs done to us forgetting this; "If you, Lord, kept a record of sins, Lord, who could stand? But with you there is forgiveness, so that we can, with reverence, serve you" (Psalm130:3-4). When we refuse to reach out and offer forgiveness to others we presume that what has been done to us is somehow far worse than anything we could have ever done. When Peter asked Jesus how many times we should forgive someone who sins against us, Jesus responded not seven times but up to seventy times seven (Matthew 18:21-22). I think His point was we shouldn't keep count at all but always be willing to forgive.

There is a beautiful story found in Luke 7 about a woman who found freedom after she realized just how much she had been forgiven. She entered the home where Jesus was, with her alabaster flask of fragrant oil, and began to wash Jesus' feet with her tears and anointed Him with oil. One of the Pharisees looked on with disgust, believing that if Jesus really was a prophet He would know that she was a sinner. The Pharisee in this story thought that his sins could never compare with the sins of the woman. However, I see nothing in the scriptures where God places our sins in degrees of "wrongness." I know there have been times when I have allowed pride to make me judge like the

Pharisee. Jesus says that if we are forgiven much we love much. I did not love much because I had the mindset that my sin wasn't as bad or as serious as someone else's might be. After all, I've never murdered anyone. I did not understand that no matter what sin I commit, when I sin against God's laws, I sin against Him. There is no escaping the fact that "all have sinned and fall short of the glory of God" (Romans 3:23). Sitting at the feet of Jesus, this woman was broken when she saw the freedom that forgiveness would bring to her life. I am arrogant in thinking that I do not need to get on my knees before the Lord and break open my alabaster box and pour out my heart of thanks to Him for all I have been forgiven.

The beauty of finding Christ's love and forgiveness is that no matter what we have done we no longer need to be tormented by our sins. When we sincerely ask for His forgiveness from our sins, He gives it. He does not hold our sins against us like most humans; in fact, He removes them "as far as the east is from the west, so far has He removed our transgressions from us" (Psalm 103:12). For all those who come to Him with a truly repentant heart, He forgives them. "For You, Lord, are good, and ready to forgive, and abundant in mercy to all those who call upon You" (Psalm 86:5). How I thank Him that He has always been ready to forgive. All I have to do is ask and then receive. The big question is, *then what?*

Freedom! When we know without a shadow of doubt that our sins have been forgiven it is absolutely possible to walk in freedom. "Because of the sacrifice of the Messiah, His blood poured out on the altar of the Cross, we're a free people—free of penalties and punishments chalked up by all our misdeeds. And not just barely free, either. Abundantly free" (Ephesians 1:7-10 The Message)! We are free to let go of bitterness, resentment and hurt. We do not need to hold on to the ugly grudges we bear. Freedom came into my heart the day that I decided to let go of all the resentments I held against those who had hurt me.

Yes, God had His children, the Israelites, and yet He saw that His family was not complete. He knew our need for Him, too. He knew that we needed a way of salvation, so He provided it. "But when the fullness of the time had come, God sent forth His Son, born of a woman, born under the law, to redeem those who were under the law, that we might receive the adoption as sons" (Galatians 4: 4-5). Just as there is a cost to adopt children here, there was a cost to God; it was His Son. What good would it do for a couple to go through the process of adoption only to have the child never acknowledge them as their parent? What would life have been like if my brother or sister never accepted our parents' last name or engaged in family life? Those who are adopted need to receive the love poured out to them from their new family. They also need to believe that everything that belongs to the parents now belongs to them. In the same way God says that "…as many as received Him, to them He gave the right to become children of God, to those who believe in His name" (John 1:12). It is in the believing and receiving of Jesus that we become a child of God. Through faith in His Son we have legal right to share in His inheritance because we have been adopted as sons (and daughters). Paul tells us in Ephesians that, "In Him also we have obtained an inheritance, being predestined according to the purpose of Him who works all things according to the counsel of His will, that we who first trusted in Christ should be to the praise of His glory" (Ephesians 1: 11-12). I love reminding myself that I am God's child. There was another bonus for my brother and sister when they came to our home; they now had a father to defend them. And we, too, as God's children, have a Heavenly Father to defend us. How tremendous it is for us that even though some of our earthly fathers may have failed in defending us we have a Heavenly Father who never will.

Years ago I volunteered at our children's elementary school as the PTA president. The committee and I needed to make an unpopular decision regarding programming we had sponsored.

One area in particular was the dance program, and we had been asked to find a new dance teacher. As you can imagine this did not go over very well with some of the parents, who did not want a change. I received many cranky phone calls and heard rampant rumors. I had heard through the rumor mill that the next PTA meeting was going to be full of irate parents. I was petrified! I began to prepare my speech and gather all my information so I could be ready to defend myself. While sitting at a stop light one morning, mentally going through my meeting agenda and defending myself to the Lord, I had a thought go running through my mind. It was more than a thought, however; it was a statement that I knew came from the Lord. It was this, "Jesus stood before Pontius Pilate and never spoke a word." Hmm, it was an interesting moment for me as I realized the truth of that statement. I was trying so hard to defend myself that it never occurred to me that I could trust God to work the situation out. I had never asked Him to be my Defender before, but I realized at that moment how badly I needed Him to be. Psalm 59:1 became my battle cry. "Deliver me from my enemies, O my God; defend me from those who rise up against me" (Psalm 59:1). You know what? It worked. No one came to the meeting that night. It was truly amazing, and it continues to amaze me each and every time I allow God to be my Defender instead of trying to do it on my own. It hasn't always been easy for me to allow God to be my Defender. There have been different instances when I have been accused, misjudged, and misunderstood, and my first inclination is to want to confront and correct. I am challenged by the example of Moses as he led the Israelites out of Egypt. When they realized the Egyptians were closing in on them and all they saw in front of them was a river, they began to accuse and question Moses's judgment in leading them away from Egypt. "And Moses said to the people, 'Do not be afraid. Stand still, and see the salvation of the Lord, which He will accomplish for you today. For the Egyptians whom you see today, you shall see again no more forever. The Lord will fight for you, and you shall hold your peace'" (Exodus 14:13-14). How many predicaments would I have saved myself from if I had only allowed the Lord to fight for me rather than trying to fight for myself?

My brother and sister received new names the day my parents signed the paperwork to adopt them. They now had American names. They became citizens of the United States, and they also became entitled to the inheritance my parents would set aside for their children one day. We, too, receive a new name, a new citizenship, and an inheritance when we accept Christ into our lives; we become children of God. Philippians 3:20 says that "… our citizenship is in heaven, from which we also eagerly wait for the Savior, the Lord Jesus Christ." I have a great inheritance through Christ. I have inherited eternal life, but I have also inherited the promises of His Word. He is my Father and my Defender. No matter what troubles we face in this life, He wants us to fight for us. "But you, God, see the trouble of the afflicted; you consider their grief and take it in hand. The victims commit themselves to you; you are the helper of the fatherless" (Psalm 10:14). Is it time you allowed yourself to truly be God's child and accept the inheritance that He has for you? Allow Him to be your Defender and Helper—and most importantly, your loving Father.

Questions to consider:

1) What do you think it means to view God as a Father?

2) What is your relationship like with your father?

3) Read 1 John 3:1-3. What are we called? What does the verse say we are to do?

4) What does verse seven of this chapter tell us to practice?

5)     Verse eight of this same chapter says he who sins is of _____

6)     We are sons of God through what according to Galatians 3:26?

7)     Galatians 3:28 says we are all what? Verse 29 says we are heirs according to what?

8)     Can you recall a time when the Lord fought for you? What happened?

9)     Read Romans 8:12-17. What does verse 14 tell us?

10)     What does Romans 8:15 remind us we did not receive? What did we receive?

# H Is for Holy

## God Says I am *Holy*

"For I am the Lord who brings you up out of the land of Egypt, to be your God. You shall therefore be *holy*, for I am *holy*."

Leviticus 11:45

*Holy*: saintly; godly; pious; devout, having a spiritually pure quality (dictionary.com, 2011).

One quiet morning as I was reading from the book of Leviticus, I read verse forty-five in chapter eleven, and a wave of shock washed over me. I read the verse again, looked up from my Bible, and said, "Lord, you expect me to be holy as *You* are holy? That's impossible! *You* are holy, and I am not." I knew I looked nothing like the image of holiness that ran through my mind, but I could not get that verse out of my mind. This seemed like such an outrageous request, but then I began to wonder why God would make a request if it were impossible to complete. I just couldn't believe that God would set us up for failure like that. So I began to ask Him for answers. Is it really possible for us to be holy as He is holy? I began to take a closer look at Leviticus and the words to His chosen people, the Israelites. I began to consider His laws and what He expected from them. I began to recognize that if He expected them to follow His laws, would He expect less from me? It was then that I realized I spent a lot of time asking Him what I should *do* with my life rather than asking Him how I should *live* my life. What would I look like if I were to live my life holy as He is holy? How would I speak, think, and behave? How would I react to all of life's situations if I were to react out of a heart filled with holiness rather than my flesh? Was He just making a wishful statement, or did He mean that we actually become holy? That seemed so unrealistic, yet the more I learned about God, the more I realized that He gave us His Word for our own good. He would not tell us to "be holy as He is holy" and not expect us to make every effort to obey those words. I truly believe that He gave us His Word with every intention that we would pursue a life of holiness for Him. I also believe He would never instruct us without giving the tools necessary to enable us in that pursuit. So if I were to pursue a life of holiness for the Lord, what changes would I need to make? Looking through the Old Testament and His laws gave me a pretty good understanding as to what I shouldn't do. I began to see that we might compromise His Word because of poor teaching, a lack of understanding, and the enticement of what the world has to offer. There were times that I would intentionally try to negotiate God's will and other times I simply did not know what the Bible said. I never spent much time reading it, and when I did I felt I did not grasp its meaning. It was a shock when I discovered Leviticus 5:17. The verse tells us, "If a person sins, and commits any of these things which are forbidden to be done by the commandments of the Lord, though he does not know it, yet he is guilty and shall bear his iniquity." We are still held accountable for sin even if we do not recognize it as such. Using the excuse, "I did not know it was wrong," isn't going to matter. I had a great revelation when I realized I could know His will for my life just by reading His Instruction Manual. If we resolve to take the time to search out the Bible, God will share His heart quite openly to reveal His desire for us on how we should live our lives. For example, in 1 Thessalonians 4:3 Paul shares, "God's will is for you to be holy…" and then he tells us one way we can accomplish this as he goes on to say, "… so stay away from all sexual sin." This is one of those areas of compromise to the world. Society and the media lead us to believe that we own our bodies, and we can do whatever we want, however we want, and with whomever we want. Well, that may be what the world wants us to believe, but God tells us differently. Holiness comes when we stay clear of all sexual sin. We must not allow the world to set our moral compass for us. God has set up boundaries for our protection and His glory. "God has called us to live holy lives, not impure lives. Therefore, anyone who refuses to live by these rules is not disobeying human teaching but is rejecting God, who gives his Holy Spirit to you" (1 Thessalonians 4:7-8). We can pray this verse from the Psalms. "Open my eyes, that I may see wondrous things from your law" (Psalm 119:18). You will see with a new set of eyes when you pray that prayer, trust me!

Excuse making was a big area of compromise for me. Too many times I allowed these thoughts to control my thinking; "It is just too hard," or, "I don't want people to think I am strange," or that big one, "What will my friends think?" Another phrase I used a lot was, "I am only human." It was just another great excuse to continue in my sin. However, if I continued to believe the lie that I could stay in sin because I was only human, then I wouldn't be able stop myself from any form of temptation. These thoughts seemed to always pop up, front and center, whenever I had a conflict between what I wanted and what I knew God wanted. Through my first Bible study I learned this great verse to help me overcome the battle of temptation. "You are tempted in the same way that everyone else is tempted. But God can be trusted not to let you be tempted too much, and He will show you how to escape from your temptations" (1 Corinthians 10:13). I just need to be willing to run for the exit door when given the chance to do so. If we are willing to listen to our Inner Man, which is the Spirit *within* us, He will show us how to escape from the temptations *around* us. Several years ago my husband's company hosted a clambake for all the employees and families. It was held shortly after we began allowing God to make changes in our lives. We had gotten back into church and we were beginning to learn more about God and His ways. We planned to enjoy the food, and I thought it might be a nice way to get to know some of his coworkers. I hadn't given a thought to the alcohol that would be available to everyone. Alcohol is not a great temptation for me. After my experience with alcohol back in high school I can not even stand the smell of it, so I do not drink.

As a group of Pat's coworkers stood in a circle chatting, one woman looked at me and said, "Kolleen, where is your drink?"

I replied, "Oh, I am fine, thanks. I had some soda."

I was caught off guard by the comments that came from this woman when she snottily replied, "Do you realize how stupid you look standing there without a drink? We all have drinks, and you are the only one who does not. You look really dumb."

I was humiliated in front of several people I did not even know. In fact, I did not know this woman very well. She just worked with my husband. With everything in me I fought the urge to go and get a cup in my hand so I could look like everyone else. I also fought tears, but I stood there and realized that this was my introduction into a life of being different from the rest. The Lord taught me that day that I was going to need to get over my "what will everyone think" mindset and realize that I needed to care more about what He thought, because as time would go on, I would discover that a life pleasing to God is a life set apart for Him. My speech and communication with others would need to change. Ephesians 5:4 taught me that foolish talk and coarse jesting is not fitting for me. So I would have to be careful now with what I said. When I think back on my life before I really believed I could change through the power of Jesus Christ I am so embarrassed. Some of my behavior was just so disgusting. I fell into the trap of believing the world rather than the Word, and I lived according to that belief. I was a very poor testimony to those around me. I believed the lie that my behavior did not matter, and the truth is, it *does* matter. It matters to God and those who are around me watching. God is counting on us, His children, to live a life that screams holiness to those who do not know Him. "Make every effort to live in peace with all men and to be holy; without holiness no one will see the Lord" (Hebrews 12:14). We must ask ourselves, "What benefit am I reaping from those things that we know are causing us shame?" (Romans 6:21). They lead us to death, and God wants us to be set free from all of that! His desire is for us to live our lives in holiness, and He can help us do it. He really will if we only allow Him. Let's ask the Holy Spirit to renew our minds so we can believe as Christ wants us to believe. We need the truth as He knows it and not as the world would want us to believe, and we can live our lives as He has called us to live them. I thank the Lord every day for His wonderful mercy and grace that allows me to walk in a new way of living! "But now having been set free from sin, and having become slaves of God, you have your fruit to holiness, and the end, everlasting life" (Romans 6:22).

Questions to consider:

1) Have you given much thought to the kind of life God has called you to live?

2) Do you believe that you can live a life of holiness? What would that look like to you and the world around you?

3) Look up the word *holy* in a thesaurus. What are some of the synonyms listed that stand out to you? Of these

words, pick one and do a word study on it. Journal what God speaks to your heart.

4) Do you remember a time when you believed you couldn't change a behavior because it was just *too hard*?

5) Think about areas in your life that you have overcome; what are they? How did you overcome them?

6) Have you ever read a verse from the Bible and thought God must have been kidding when He wrote it?

7) Do a word study and find scriptures that tell you more of what God's will is for you.

8) What are we encouraged to do in Ephesians 5:10?

# I Is for Image

## God Says I Am Made in His *Image*

"So God created man in his own *image*, in the *image* of God he created him; male and female he created them."

Genesis 1:27

*Image*: a physical likeness or representation of a person, animal, or thing, photographed, painted, sculptured, or otherwise made visible (dictionary.com, 2011).

One of my favorite hobbies is photography. I love looking through the lens of a camera and trying to capture a story through the image before me. I am always amazed when I look at the photograph and I see the image before me because it looks a little different when captured by my camera than what I saw with my natural eye. There is clarity, and the photo is in finer detail. Sometimes I get frustrated when the picture is a little out of focus, and an area I did not even notice is sharp and clear. Recently I participated in a few photo courses and discovered that I love having my instructors comment on the pictures I submit. They have an eye for catching details and ways I could improve the photo. My instructors have taught me ways to enhance my pictures that I had never before considered. I learned several years ago that I also needed to allow God to become the Instructor in my life. God has a way of catching areas that are a little out of focus in my life, places I seem to overlook or ignore, and pointing out what needs some adjustment. With today's computer programs it is easy to just Photoshop away entire negative details in a photograph. Those five pounds that found me—Gone! The wrinkles on my face and the dark circles under my eyes—Gone! Each and every negative aspect of the photo that I do not like can easily be removed with a few clicks of the button. If only the changes God wanted to see in me were as easy to complete! Unfortunately, when it comes to changing the actual image that everyone else may see, it takes work. If I want to lose those five pounds, I am going to have to exercise and eat right to do it. The same is true when God begins to bring into focus the areas He wants to adjust in my life. I appreciate that He shows us little by little, and little by little He began to zero in on the image I had of myself. He wanted me to realize that my focus was off.

Before I knew Christ I based my self-worth on wrong things, not His image. This statement I read from *The Handbook of Bible Application* brought new revelation to me, and God used it to change my way of thinking:

> Knowing that we are made in God's image and thus share many of His characteristics provides a solid basis for self-worth. Human worth is not based on possessions, achievements, physical attractiveness or public acclaim. Instead it is based on being made in God's image. Because we bear God's image, we can feel positive about ourself. Criticizing or downgrading ourself is criticizing what God has made and the abilities He has given us. Knowing that you are a person of worth helps you to love God, know Him personally and make a valuable contribution to those around you.
>
> The Handbook of Bible Application

As someone who was called to be a stay-at-home mom I can relate to the need to find my self-worth not from *what* I was doing but from the fact that I was made in God's image. One day while my husband and I sat talking with friends the wife made a comment that hurt me deeply. She is now retired, but she had been a working mom, and she began to talk about me being "an anchor around my husband's neck." In her mind, because I did not work outside the home and contribute financially, I was no more than a heavy weight for my husband to bear. I was crushed by those words and it took quite a while for me to get over the hurt of that statement. For many years after that I used to say, "I am a mother, a wife, a daughter, a sister, and a friend," but I did not really know who Kolleen was. Who is Kolleen, the person, and what is her purpose? I have known many people who have searched high and low to find the answer to that question for themselves. Often times, I believe, we never really discover who we are because we are trying to portray an image of who we think we need to be. After our friend made the statement about me, I really felt very little self-worth. After all, I really wasn't contributing much to the world...I was just a stay-at-home mom. (Forget the fact that I was molding the lives of our children!) It took God much convincing—and my taking many jobs that I knew I shouldn't take—to get me to the place where I am now. I now understand that my self-worth is not in what I *do*, but my self-worth needs to come from the fact that I am made in the image of God. And because I am made in His image I then needed to discover what that looked like. If the definition of image is a physical likeness or representation of someone, then how does one represent Christ? I began to seek the answer to that question, and the answer, I discovered, was found by spending time with Him. When we spend time with people we tend to act like them and pick up habits and mannerisms. We may look at those we associate with and think about ways we want to be more like them. Spend too much time with a negative, depressed, bitter person, and it won't be long before you see life through their eyes. Hang out with someone who loves life and finds good in everything, and pretty soon you will, too.

The Lord began to show me that being made in His image meant that I was a reflection of His character. Soon I was able to find contentment and feel complete because I began to find my worth in Him. It took time, but I stopped allowing others to make me feel less because I wasn't doing what *they* thought I should be doing. I became more confident in myself as a person, knowing that God made me who I am for the purpose of serving Him—not man. I was not put here to find my self-worth through the opinion of others. *The Handbook of Bible Application* goes on to say,

> We are all created by God, in His image and while we were made in His image we will never be exactly like Him, because He is our supreme Creator. But we do have the ability to reflect His character in our love, patience, forgiveness, kindness and faithfulness.

What were we created to do? *Reflect God's character* to others. One of the first characteristics of God I began to study came from reading 1 John 4:16. "And we have known and believed the love that God has for us. *God is love*, and he who abides in love abides in God, and God in him" (*emphasis added*). Once I read that I understood being made in God's image meant that I needed to abide in His love. He is love; I needed to also *be* love. Love needed to flow from me in the same way it would flow from Him. It only made sense for me to get into the Word and discover what a person abiding in His love might look like. The perfect chapter to learn about love is called "The Love Chapter." Through the verses in 1 Corinthians 13 the Lord began to teach me and show me His character. If God is love then God is described through these verses.

> Love is patient, love is kind. It does not envy, it does not boast, it is not proud. It does not dishonor others, it is not self-seeking, it is not easily angered, it keeps no record of wrongs. Love does not delight in evil but rejoices with the truth. It always protects, always trusts, always hopes, always perseveres.
>
> 1 Corinthians 13: 4-7

I once heard a speaker say that if you wanted to walk in love, take out the word *love* and put your name in its place. So I began to do just that, and I would repeat this over and over. It especially came in handy when I was upset over something someone said or a hurt that was trying to take root in my heart. If I was growing impatient with my children I would speak out, "Kolleen is patient. Kolleen is kind." If I was struggling with jealousy or envy I would say, "Kolleen does not envy. Kolleen is not proud, etc." It was life changing. I was altering how I viewed myself, and as I did that I was able to change how I responded to situations in my life. When I handled a situation with patience, or I did not allow myself to fly off the handle easily, I was pleasantly surprised (as were those who knew me!). I came to realize that being made in God's image meant that I was going to learn how to speak kindly to people, how to not take offense easily, and I was going to learn to love others even when it was hard. I have a very powerful voice (that's a nice way of saying *big mouth*), and at times people would think I was mad when I said something because it could come out sounding sharp. I always felt harassed for my loudness, so I had to allow God to show me how to speak differently. I also had to learn that sometimes I did not even need to speak.

It became a fervent prayer of mine that the Lord would help me grow and mature in love and in my reflection of His love for others. But we will not reflect His love to others without accepting it for ourselves first. God desires for us to understand this so we can know contentment. Far too many of us are striving toward success from the world's perspective and not from understanding His love for us and our need for Him. When we believe that we are a person of worth, not only can we admire our similarities, but we will also be able celebrate our differences knowing that each one of us, male and female, are created equal in *His image*. We will no longer feel the need to compete against each other, criticize others, or even ourselves. We bear the image of God, and because we will made in His image, criticizing ourselves or others is actually criticizing God.

I recently had a woman share a story with me about a time she was on the worship team at her church. While at a worship conference, members were asked to compare each individual with a disciple of Jesus. Innocently, this woman told someone that she reminded her of Peter. Rather than ask her why she saw her as Peter, the woman became offended and insulted at the comparison. So great was her resentment that she slipped out of church for months because she did not want to risk running into this woman. She allowed the offense to fester in her heart until she finally felt she was able to confront her "sister in the Lord." So one Sunday, following church, she walked up to the woman and began to share her offended heart with her. Six months of allowing an offense to fester in her heart came pouring out all over the other woman. And in her closing statement she told her, "I haven't been able to attend church for the past six months because watching you on the worship team makes me want to throw up." She tore this woman apart with accusations and assumptions, and when she was finished with her tirade she waited. Shocked and confused, the other woman, who because so much time had passed couldn't even remember the situation, simply apologized.

And when she apologized the offended woman responded, "Wow, I did not know you were so approachable." She could have saved herself six months of suffering if she had simply gone to the woman the moment she felt the sting of offense hit her. And she would have spared the other woman the hurt and embarrassment of the confrontation.

Yes, we are told in the scriptures to go to one another if we have been offended. But too many times we are confronting out of our own anger and hurt. We use the scriptures to justify our telling someone all we feel they have done to wrong us. We can say it is out of love that we go to a person, but when we pull out a four-page letter of accusations and begin to list in detail every error committed, well, I just do not see any love in that. And I do not see God in it, either. God has never crushed me with cruel words that have left me wounded like the dead. He has always come to me in love with the grace to change. I have had people come to me and say, "God sent me to tell you..." and then crush me with accusations and assumptions. I have also been confronted by people in whom I truly saw the image of God reflected in them because of their concern to come to me in love out of obedience to the Lord. As sisters in Christ we must stop our criticism of one another. We must stop taking offense with each other and learn to trust that God can help us overcome miscommunication and insults. If a statement was made that you took offense to, first ask God to show you why it offended you. Are you being overly sensitive? I could not begin to tell you how many times the Lord has told me to let something go because I was being too sensitive. He has taught me the importance of believing the best of people, not the worst. Sometimes comments made can come across differently than how it was meant, so believe the best in one another. If you really must go to the person about the statement because you can not get over it, then please do. But can I suggest that you ask them to forgive you first for harboring the bitterness toward them for the offense. You may say something like, "I may have taken it wrong, but it was hurtful, and I have carried an offense against you because of it. Please forgive me." I am aware now that many times I become offended because of pride.

Pride can bring me down if I am not careful, so I need to mind my reactions. I ask myself when I have acted ugly toward someone if God is wondering, *Do I really look like that? Is that how people really see me? Better yet, is that truly a proper representation of who I AM?*

I bear God's image, and because I bear His image I must do everything I can to walk in a manner worthy of this. If this means I need to not speak, I will learn to hold my tongue. If it means that I must humble myself and believe the best of my sister who just made a remark that stung me, then I will bring it to the Lord and ask Him to help me overcome it. I want to reflect Him well to those around me inside the church as well as outside of it. What about you? Will you lay down your offenses, your critical spirit, and your bitterness toward whoever has offended you and allow others to see God's image through you? It is time to seek God's character in our own lives so we can become a physical representation of Him on earth, seeking to pour out love, patience, forgiveness, kindness, and faithfulness to everyone around us.

Questions to consider:

1) Why do you think we must know we are a person of worth in order for us to love God, know Him personally, and make a valuable contribution to those around us?

2) Would you say you have a good, healthy self-image, or do you think of yourself as someone with low self-esteem?

3) Look up Proverbs 19:11. What can we learn from this verse?

4) Read Colossians 3: 2. Where are we supposed to focus our thoughts—on spiritual things or earthly things?

5) In verse 5 of Colossians 3, we are told to "put to death whatever belongs to your earthly nature." What do you need to put to death?

6) Find three scriptures that describe God's character and list them.

7) What characteristics of God's image do you think you portray pretty well now? Which do you need to work on?

8) How have you been hurt by another's unkind words? Will you choose to forgive?

9) Do you have a secure understanding that you were made in God's image?

10) How can the church become more like Christ within the church body?

# J Is for Justified

## God Says I am *Justified*

"Therefore let it be known to you, brethren, that through this Man is preached to you the forgiveness of sins; and by Him everyone who believes is *justified* from all things from which you could not be justified by the law of Moses."

Acts 13: 38-39

*Justified*: to declare innocent or guiltless; absolve; acquit (dictionary.com, 2011).

*Absolve*: to free from guilt or blame or their consequences (dictionary.com, 2011).

I once had a conversation with a woman who said that she believed in God but struggled with the forgiveness of sins aspect of Christianity. Her belief is that people use faith in Christ as a way to do whatever they want and then say, "Oh, I am a Christian, and I am forgiven of that." She feels that there are far too many people who use the "I am forgiven" card as a way to justify wrong behavior. Do whatever you want, and when you get caught bring out your forgiven card and pass go. One example she shared with me is the resentment she feels towards a woman who, years ago, had an affair with a married man. The two divorced their spouses and married each other, and since that time they have become strong believers in Christ. She cannot grasp in her mind how people can claim that God can forgive any and all sin. Two families were split up because of infidelity. I can certainly understand her dilemma in this area. When we turn on our televisions and hear stories of abuse and scandal it can be hard to understand that God will forgive any sin. She, like so many of us, believes that there must be a price to pay for our actions and to say that God forgives any wrong action is scandalous in itself. But God's gift of absolving us from our sin is not about justifying wrong behavior; it is really about being justified *from* the wrong behavior.

That is what the Bible is all about. It is the story of redemption. It is the story of a God who loves us and made a way for us to be free from the bondage of our sin. We can read the Bible and see broken people who made mistakes and a God who would reach out in pure love to save them. He brought salvation to us through His one and only Son, Jesus. That all who believe in Jesus would be justified from all things. He gave His law, but the law couldn't bring forgiveness for sins. Jesus brought that. And when He died He made it possible for us to become justified before God. While it is true that there was a sin debt I owed to God that I could not pay, Jesus became that payment so I could find forgiveness and eternal life. "For the wages of sin is death, but the free gift of God is eternal life in Christ Jesus our Lord" (Romans 6:23). I believe that when we refuse to let go of sin, or refuse to believe we are forgiven for our sin, we are insulting what Jesus did for us on the cross. The Greek translation of the word justified is *dikaioō* and it means: to declare, pronounce, one to be just, righteous, or such as he ought to be (Strongs, Blueletterbible.org, 1996-2011). "Such as he ought to be"—now that is a seed we should take and plant deep into our hearts and allow those words to take root and grow within us. We are not living *such as we ought to be* when we refuse to believe in the power of God's forgiveness. What did He send His Son for if we aren't going to believe that we can be forgiven?

In our human thinking we believe you must pay over and over and over for your sins. We never want to let anyone off the hook. How many times do people bring up past mistakes in a confrontation with someone? Never allowing the person to forget the sins of their past. If we are living out of our natural self, that's what we do. But if we are living out of our spiritual self we understand that God does not do that, and neither should we. God tells us that when we repent our sins have been removed from us as far as the east is from the west. Or as the Message Bible says it, "And as far as sunrise is from sunset, He has separated us from our sins" (Psalm 103:12). We must learn to let people off the hook, and we must realize that it is ok to let ourselves off the hook, too. Once we repent from a sincere heart the sin we committed is under Christ's blood, and we become justified before God. Every time we refuse to let go of our own guilt for a sin we have asked forgiveness for, we are telling Jesus His death wasn't enough. I was so convicted by this when the Lord spoke this truth to my heart.

There were times when I allowed my mind to take a trip back into history and review all the mistakes of my past. It is funny how that happens. Suddenly a thought would sneak into my mind and before long I could physically feel the pressing weight of my sins on me. The thoughts of what I had done, the hurts I have caused others, the shamefulness of it all would wash over me, and that's all I could think about. It also would cause fear to grip me. What if God really does not forgive me? How can He when I could not even forgive myself? When I allowed my thoughts to wander I began to wonder how I could ever be forgiven. I would get caught up in the realization of the horrible person I really was. Guilt and shame would become my new best friends, and before I knew it I was so full of condemnation I barely functioned. I would become depressed and feel rejected. I can become consumed with myself and eat my way through a day. Then God, in His mercy, gave me new understanding when I read this:

> Then I heard a loud voice saying in heaven, "Now salvation, and strength, and the kingdom of our God, and the power of His Christ have come, for the accuser of our brethren, who accused them before our God day and night, has been cast down" (Revelation 12:10).

Satan is the accuser of the brethren. He brings the accusations to our minds. When I begin to travel the "wander and wonder path," as I like to call it, the accusations and guilt begin to grow. Or when my thoughts turn in the direction of, *Look at what you've done*, or, *How could you?* Or, *How could God forgive you?* Or, *If people only knew what you really were like*, it is at that moment that I need to remind myself that God does not accuse—Satan does. God is full of grace and mercy. He convicts, and there is a difference between the two. Conviction is when He begins to impress upon me an area that needs attention. Accusations are fault-finding and full of blame that lead to condemnation. We must learn to recognize the difference between the voice of the accuser and the voice of the Holy Spirit. Memorizing Romans 8:1 can certainly help us fight the battle of condemnation.

"There is therefore now no condemnation to those who are in Christ Jesus, who do not walk according to the flesh, but according to the Spirit" (Romans 8:1).

Satan does not just bring accusations before God; he also brings accusations to our minds about one another. That is a good thing to remember when we refuse to let someone off the hook for a failure in their life. When I begin to think about how a friend has let me down or how they have appeared to have failed me, or when my mind wanders to a place that brings up accusations against another, I must be quick to recognize the direction my thoughts are taking me. Satan accuses us before God and before one another. If your mind is focused on how horrible the person is or that action was, then you are listening to the accuser. The Word says he accuses night and day. He never stops. Have you ever been around a person who just would not stop talking about an issue they had? I can be that way. If I have a point to make and I feel as though you're not getting my point, I will go on and on until you do. I wonder if God ever looks at Satan and just wishes He could say, "Enough already! Just be quiet!" I've seen that look on my husband's face a time or two.

You may be thinking, *Yes, but you do not know what I've done; God could never forgive me.* Maybe you have been involved in a scandal of your own. Be encouraged because God is a God of the new thing. He likes to breathe new life into a dead one. He is a God of restoration and resurrection. He says, "Do not remember the former things, nor consider the things of old. Behold, I will do a new thing, now it shall spring forth; shall you not know it? I will even make a road in the wilderness and rivers in the desert" (Isaiah 43:18 & 19).

When we have the faith to believe that God is able to forgive all sins then we must begin to live like it. We do not dwell on our past mistakes and let the guilt of our failures swallow us up and consume us. We live like the justified people we are. We do not accuse ourselves or others. We can say one thing but our actions tell another story. God wants us to know that "He who covers his sins will not prosper, but whoever confesses and forsakes them will have mercy" (Proverbs 28:13). As far as the couple I mentioned earlier, yes, it was a very sad thing that happened between them and they truly have repented for the pain of an affair. People are hurt by sin, and our choices do have consequences that we will live out. But they accepted the freedom that Jesus offered to them to let go of guilt and shame through faith in what He accomplished on the cross. They realize that they now can stand before God *justified* because Jesus took that sin upon Himself. They could never *work* hard enough for that forgiveness. They needed faith in Christ to overcome that. "Therefore we conclude that a man is justified by faith apart from the deeds of the law" (Romans 3:28).

I find it interesting in so many ways that I can justify just about anything. I can justify why I need to buy that new outfit, why I need to eat that last piece of chocolate cake, why I absolutely have to have a new car, why I have every right to be mad at the person who hurt me, and why I am right and my husband is wrong! I can even justify the sin in my life and why I cannot let it go, but I have a hard time justifying why I should be "declared innocent or guiltless" or live as I ought to be as a child of God. The very best way for me to remember that through the sacrifice of Jesus I can stand before God innocent, absolved from, or free from the guilt of all my sins is to remember the definition of justified this way "just as if I'd never sinned." Now, let's go live like it.

Questions to consider:

1)  Do you know people, like my friend, who believe people use freedom in *faith* as a basis for doing wrong things and then claim forgiveness for it?

2)  Some might say that there is no way God can forgive all sins. Some are just too horrible. Do you think He forgives *all* sin? Can you find a scripture to verify this?

3)  Do you think knowing God will forgive us and forget our sins means we can do whatever we want? What does 1 Corinthians 6:12 say about this?

4)  Have you ever lost sight of what Jesus accomplished for you at the cross?

5)  Read through Matthew 27. What are your thoughts as you read through it?

6)   Read Romans 4:1-3. Was Abraham justified through works or faith?

7)   Why do you think it is easier to justify sin in our lives, make excuses for holding onto it, than it is to allow God to set us free from it?

8)   Can you think of things you justify in your life that are considered sin in God's eyes?

9)   What can you learn from reading Romans 5:8-10?

10)  1 John 1:9 says what?

#  Is for Known

## God Says He *Knows* Me

"O Lord, You have searched me and *known* me."

Psalm 139:1

*Know*: be acquainted with (a thing, place, person, etc.), as by sight, experience, or report (dictionary.com, 2011).

Over the last twenty-eight years of marriage we have attended six churches. I know that may seem like a lot, especially if you have attended the same church your entire life. But I believe that God moves you to grow you, and it is important to be flexible and allow Him to place you where He wants you. There may be different reasons why He would move you from one church to another. I recognize now that He moved us out of one church because the teaching was off scripturally. He moved us out of one church after a time of training to serve in another, and He took us from the place of serving to a place of rest and healing. Unfortunately, I can look back and see a time when we left a church because of a grievance against a new pastor. I'm still not exactly sure why he and I did not get along, but we did not. In all honesty now, though, I will admit that much of it was due to my immaturity as a Christian. I am not proud of it, but I am not too proud to admit it, either. Now I appreciate the fact that the

84

Lord allowed me to leave a church mad and connected me with a pastor who saw the immaturity in me and allowed God to show him that I was worth investing in.

As I look back now I can say that this was one of the most blessed times, and yet one of the most excruciatingly painful times of my life. The first two years I spent at this church were spent crying. It was here that I discovered what death to self really meant. God had taken me, a bulldozer, and put me under the leadership of a pastor who was more like a hand shovel. With my very choleric personality it was easy for me to bulldoze my way through each day. I have said it before, and it bears repeating; I like things my own way, and I have a very natural way of controlling things. If there happened to be a dirt pile in my way I would bulldoze my way through. But my pastor was a very gentle man who was much more careful about where and how he chose to turn over the dirt. I am so thankful that he was. He began the process of digging deep into my heart and helped me see what made me tick. He taught me the importance of allowing someone to dig around in areas that you want to remain hidden. Secrets are like mold inside of us; left alone in the dark they begin to spread and contaminate other areas. We like to keep secrets hidden away, but there is such freedom in releasing them. He taught me a valuable life lesson when he showed me that my past was to be a place of reference, not a place of residence. Living in the past does not allow God the freedom to move us into the future He has planned for us. If we are always looking behind us, we are not able to look forward to our future. I had come into the church carrying lots of extra baggage. There was the hurt of a broken friendship and the extra baggage leaving a church with a grievance brings. You do not just leave a church if you are leaving for the wrong reasons. If you cannot leave with the pastor's blessing then whatever issues you have there will follow you to the next one. God used our pastor to help restore healing and forgiveness in both relationships. God also used him to bring out gifts and talents in me that I never even knew were there. It was during my time here that God revealed the Beatitudes to me for the first time. One in particular jumped out at me. "Blessed are the pure in heart for they shall see God" (Matthew 5:8). God was able to set my heart free because of a pastor who was willing to say hard things to me. God knew the person He created me to be, and He knew exactly who it was that could help me discover my true identity at this point of the journey. I had learned how important it was to move with God. I also began to recognize it was equally important that my motives be right regarding the decisions that I made.

I began to see that God was searching me out, and nothing I did was going to go unnoticed by Him. My actions and attitude were under His microscope for sure. One of the Greek translations of the word *searched* is *investigate* (Strong's, H2713). I certainly could relate to the fact that I felt as though I was always under His investigation. He was actively investigating me and He knew when the decisions I made were based on my desire to bring glory to Him or to myself. There were many times that I believed my motives were pure in my decisions, but Proverbs 16:2 points out that, "All a person's ways seem pure to them, but motives are weighed by the Lord." The truth behind the motive always became clear when I was willing to listen to the Holy Spirit ask me a very simple question. "Why?"

In Genesis 37 we read the story of Jacob and his twelve sons, one of whom is Joseph. I've always read this story and focused on Joseph and how God was with him through the years he spent in Egypt. But one day the Lord twisted my view a little and pointed out the brothers. This day I saw the story of eleven brothers who turn against the younger brother, throw him into a pit, and then decide to sell him to Midianite traders passing by. Then they return to their father with the boy's coat dipped in goat's blood and allow him to believe that his son has been killed. How could these brothers keep the secret of what really happened to Joseph from their father? How could they have watched him mourn the loss of a son and not speak up? Well, I believe they had some issues against Joseph and their dad. We read first that Joseph was seen as a tattletale. He had taken a bad report to dad about the boys in the field (Genesis 37:2). The father played favorites, loving Joseph more than the others because he was the son of his old age (Genesis 37:3). This, as you can imagine, did not sit well with his brothers. And it got to the point "…when his brothers saw that their father loved him more than all his brothers, they hated him and could not speak peaceably to him" (Genesis 37:4). Watching your father pour out his favor on one of your brothers can certainly inflict pain and can easily cause division. As if that wasn't enough, Joseph poured salt in their wound when he had a dream, "and when he told the dream to his brothers they hated him even more" (verse 5). Years later Joseph would confront the motive in their hearts when he spoke, "But as for you, you meant evil against me; but God meant it for good, in order to bring it about as it is this day, to save many people alive." (Genesis 50:20). Their motive was to simply be rid of him because of the jealousy they harbored toward him. Our actions will reflect the motives of our hearts.

We might have a situation in our own life that seems too hard to deal with, too painful to confront, so we try to find a way to escape it. Maybe you can relate to the brothers having a sense that another sibling can do no wrong, so you remove yourself from your family. It is just too painful. We might move from the neighborhood, change jobs, change spouses, or like me, change churches because it is easier to run than to confront the actual motive behind our hurt. Husbands and wives divorce one another with all types of excuses as to why they could not stay in the marriage without ever looking deep enough to uncover the real motive behind the desire to leave. Girls will get pregnant to keep a boyfriend, and a guy might use threats and abuse to hold onto his girl. A lady at the office befriends a male coworker with one motive in mind—to make him hers. We really have no problem these days convincing ourselves that we are entitled to have anything we want, and whatever we must do to obtain it is fine, too. I would like to add here, too, that it does matter what we wear. It does matter how low and how tight. Do not be fooled into believing that it does not. Asking yourself before you walk out the door, "What am I drawing attention to…and why?" is a very important question. While we can try to justify our actions to those around us, and we may even try to ignore them, we must remember that we cannot hide our true motives from the Lord. "God is in charge of human life, watching and examining us inside and out" (Proverbs 20:27, MSG).

Through the years I have learned that when facing decisions, I must check my motives because God cares about them, and He wants my heart to be pure. I ask Him all the time to show me what my true motives are in a situation. If I am angry about something, I need to ask Him to show me what I am really angry about and what the motive behind the anger is. Most of the time anger comes out of a hurt. So why am I hurt? We can learn a great deal from this passage about conflict that happens when our motives aren't right.

> What is causing the quarrels and fights among you? Don't they come from the evil desires at war within you? You want what you don't have, so you scheme and kill to get it. You are jealous of what others have, but you could not get it, so you fight and wage war to take it away from them. Yet you don't have what you want because you don't ask God for it. And even when you ask, you don't get it because your motives are all wrong—you want only what will give you pleasure.
>
> James 4:2-3

Recognizing that God knows me best helps me understand that His ways will always bring the best for me out of any situation.

You know my sitting down and my rising up; You understand my thought afar off. You comprehend my path and my lying down, and are acquainted with all my ways. For there is not a word on my tongue, but behold, O LORD, You know it altogether.

Psalm 139:2-4

Psalm 139 helps us to recognize that He knew each and every one of us before we were born. All the days for us have been written in His book for us to complete. Ask Him to search you and know your heart. Ask Him to show you your anxieties and see if there is any wicked way in you. Then ask Him to lead you into the way everlasting!

Questions to consider:

1) Why do you think people run from conflict rather than confront it?

2) Do you have a hard time with conflict?

3) Can you think of a time when you walked away from a situation rather than allow healthy confrontation?

4) God is into figuring us out when we don't really understand ourselves. Do you allow God to "actively investigate" your heart, or do you shut yourself off from that?

5) Read 1 Chronicles 28:9. What advice did David have for Solomon? What did he tell him about the Lord?

6)  Have you ever struggled with jealousy toward another? How do you handle jealousy in yourself? Do you recognize it as such?

7)  Has God ever taken what someone meant for evil against you and turned it to good? What happened?

8)  Have you ever considered how intimately it is that you are known by God?

9)  When a situation happens that makes you angry, have you ever stopped to ask yourself, "What is the real issue behind the anger?"

10) Read Psalm 139. List all He knows about you.

11) Make Psalm 139: 23-24 your heart's prayer.

# L Is for LOVED

## God Says I am *Loved*

"For I am convinced that neither death nor life, neither angels nor demons, neither the present nor the future, nor any powers, neither height nor depth, nor anything else in all creation, will be able to separate us from the *love* of God that is in Christ Jesus our Lord."

Romans 8:38 & 39

*Love*: a profoundly tender, passionate affection for another person. A feeling of warm personal attachment or deep affection, as for a parent, child, or friend (dictionary.com, 2011).

I've come to realize that there is one experience that happens in life that I do not really care for. It is the pain separation can bring. Our children have grown up and moved out, and now we are separated by distance, and honestly I do not like it much. I would love to have them live close enough to us for Sunday dinners and a visit whenever I wanted. Our extended families live all over the country, so getting together with all the family takes an event like a wedding or, unfortunately, a funeral. Even then some might not be able to attend. We know from experience the grief and sorrow that the separation of death causes. We have witnessed the pain of watching close friends separate after years of marriage. I know first hand the pain felt by the separation of friendships. Even watching our children break off a relationship has caused pain in the process. With each of these types of separations it is easy to mull the "if only" statement over and over in our thinking. *If only* our kids could find closer jobs. *If only* our family could live closer. *If only* I understood why. *If only* we could redo the day we lost our loved one. There are many of us who would love to have the chance to redo a day. We have a tendency to live in the "if only" when it comes to the memory of that day and that can put sorrow and regret into our hearts. The pain of separation is bad enough but add to it the pain of regret, and it is a heavy burden to carry. I have carried rejection at times when a friendship has gone sour. That's why I am overcome with immense gratitude when I read the above verse from Romans. Discovering we have the promise that nothing can ever separate us from the love of God was a great comfort to me. It should be to you, too. We endure far too many separations as it is; what would we ever do if we had to worry about God removing His love from us? Unfortunately for me there were many times when I lived in doubt of that promise. I struggled with the truth of that scripture because for a long time I had a belief that I needed to earn His love. And honestly, when I endured the sting of rejection by a close friend, I began to wonder how I could trust that God would always love me. This can become another area in which it is far too easy to live with the question of "if only." *If only* I were a better friend, or *if only* I were a better person, then we might still be friends. I began to put that same attitude onto God. *If only* I worked a little harder or if I could act better; *if only* I were good enough then I could earn God's love and acceptance. How blessed and fortunate we are that even though we might want to believe that, God never said that.

For many years I thought that once I failed God through sin, or let Him down by an act of disobedience, then I had to work to earn His love back. It would take me a long time to believe that I had paid my dues for my sinful act. I assumed that with extra hard work and trying to be perfect, then I might get back in the good graces of God. Through the years I have had numerous conversations with women who have expressed the same struggle. We all want to believe that it takes hard work to earn God's love. What I finally discovered was that I behave as I believe and my belief was in a love that was very conditional. And if I am a person who does not love unconditionally I am going to have a hard time believing that God, or anyone, loves me unconditionally. I understood that God's love was conditional because my love was conditional. What I found was God's love is far more pure than the love that is so misunderstood today. We place conditions on the love we give to others. I was consumed with a love that is full of gush and mush, you know, the feel-good stuff—the love that is all about me. If I wasn't feeling good that day the love bank was closed. I could pull out my "if only" list and use it to make sure those around me were working hard to meet my needs. But God never based His love on a to-do list. His love was never based on my works or my doing everything right. It was simply based on who He is and the fact that He simply loved me for me—pure and simple love because God is Love.

It was all about love when He chose the Israelites as His inheritance. It was all about love for His people when He delivered them out of Egypt. It was all about love when He wrote out His commandments for His children to follow. It was all about love when He, unconditionally, gave His Son for *all* mankind. "For God *so loved* the world that He gave his one and only Son, that whoever believes in Him shall not perish but have eternal life" (John 3:16). He did not do it just for those who were doing everything right but for an entire world. He did it for those who would accept the gift He offered knowing that there would be some who rejected the gift. Once I was able to understand that my performance does not warrant whether God's love remained, I was able to see that I needed to stop placing conditions on those around me. The Lord helped me recognize that manipulating others for my benefit is not love. It was easy for me to shower those around me with love if things were going my way. If my kids were obeying me and not challenging the rules, if I was feeling good about myself, or my husband and friends were meeting my needs, then love freely flowed. It is always easy to give love when I am getting my way. But watch out if I was challenged in any way. Good-bye, love, hello, silent treatment, cold shoulder and guilt trip! You see, I was forgetting that no one should have to work to earn my love. God does not base His love for me on my behavior, so why would I base my love on the behavior of those around me? He has never based His love on the behavior of His people, and that is a good thing.

When I read through the Old Testament I learn so much about the love of God toward a people whose behavior might not have warranted it. (It is a good thing I wasn't the one calling the shots with them; there is no telling how things would have turned out!) While He continued to pour out love they continued to pour out complaints, accusations, and rebellion. Because of His unconditional love, instead of turning against them He continued in His covenant with them. Did He ever become frustrated and angry with them? Yes, He did. He became so angry with them at one point He wanted to disinherit them. But the Israelites were to discover what Psalm 30:5 reminds us. "For His anger lasts only a moment, but His favor lasts a lifetime." The cool thing about God is this; He never shuts off the love valve. It was always flowing even in His anger. One of my favorite words of the Bible is the word *nevertheless* found in Psalms 106. This Psalm recaps the journey of the Israelites and the Lord's mercy. We learn that the Israelites rebelled against Him, forgot Him, and tested Him. They envied Moses and Aaron; they worshipped the golden calf and defiled the land. They forgot God was their Savior. The list is long, and His wrath was kindled against them, but twice we see this word, nevertheless.

"Nevertheless He saved them for His name's sake, That He might make His mighty power known" (Psalm 106:8).

"Nevertheless He regarded their affliction, when He heard their cry; and for their sake He remembered His covenant, and relented according to the multitude of His mercies" (Psalm 106:44-45).

Nevertheless is a sweet reminder that *in spite of* all that I do He still says nothing can separate me from His love—nothing. Oh, there have been times when I have been tempted to believe that when the Lord seems distant it is because I have done something that caused Him to stop loving me. But I have heard it said many times that when God seems distant from us He is not the One who moved. Sin causes separation, not from His love but from Him. A holy God and sin do not mix, and when I sin I have broken my union with Him. Thankfully He does not deal with us according to our sins or what we deserve, and in His mercy He disciplines us. Just as there were times that He disciplined the Israelites and He never stopped loving them, in the same way He will never stop loving me even when He needs to discipline me. That's an area I was very weak in understanding. When I was disciplined I always took it as rejection. But God has shown me there is actually great love in being disciplined and corrected. And within the world we live today we have a hard time understanding that.

There is a huge misconception when it comes to love and discipline. Because we do not understand what real love looks like, we also do not know what loving discipline looks like. Parents are afraid to bring correction or discipline to children nowadays because we are afraid they will think we do not love them. Or we go to the other extreme, and what we call discipline is actually *abuse*. It was never easy to discipline our children when they were young. But we saw early on as new parents that whatever our children thought they could get away with they were going to try. At times it may have been easier to overlook each and every transgression, but we had the best interest of our children in mind. It was important for our children to understand that our discipline came from our hearts of love for them. We wanted them to know that boundaries are in place for good reason—their protection. If you cross a boundary line that has been put in place to protect you, chances are good that you are going to get hurt. So when we would see our children begin to cross that boundary line we would try to get their attention through a warning. If they did not listen to the warning then we needed to take action, and sometimes the discipline that followed was painful for them.

God has shown me in the same way that He has a boundary line in place for us, too. It is a place of protection and safety. When I cross that line He is going to get my attention in order to keep me from straying too far. As God's spokesman, Moses was sent to the Israelites with instructions along with many warnings. But when the Israelites rebelled against Him in the wilderness and continued to test Him, He took away their entrance into the Promised Land. He forgave them and still loved them, but that generation lost the right to enter the land promised to their fathers. We must be very careful that we do not allow pride to keep us from hearing the Lord's warnings when they come. There have been times in my life when God would bring someone to speak a word of warning to me because I was in disobedience. Sometimes I would heed the warning, but other times I just got mad and refused to listen. I had a very hard time hearing what I did not want to hear. Proverbs 19:20 is a very important verse to remember. "Listen to advice and accept discipline, and at the end you will be counted among the wise" (Proverbs 19:20). We are in pride when we choose not to listen godly counsel, and God hates pride. His love runs deep for us, and He will send a warning when necessary. We must be careful that we heed the warnings. None of us are immune from His discipline. We need to find security in knowing "…that as a man disciplines his son, so the Lord your God disciplines you" (Deuteronomy 8:4). Discipline is never fun to endure, but we can learn from Hebrews 12 that, "No discipline seems pleasant at the time, but painful. Later on, however, it produces a harvest of righteousness and peace for those who have been trained by it" (Hebrews 12:11).

We need to be careful that we do not accept a standard of discipline that differs from how God intended. He is balanced; we need to be balanced, too. And do not be afraid of the Lord's discipline, for "Those whom I love I rebuke and discipline. So be earnest and repent" (Revelation 3:19).

I may still say *if only* every now and then when it comes to wanting my family to be closer, but I will never again believe that *if only* applies to my needing to work harder or do better to earn the Lord's love. Instead, the word *nevertheless* will come from my lips when I have flubbed things up and I want to look at how I failed. If God can say it, then I will, too. Nevertheless is a much better word, don't you agree?

Questions to consider:

1) Read Psalm 106. What does verse three tell you?

2) What does verse seven tell us about the Israelites?

3) Verses 9 through 11 tell us what He did for them. What was it?

4) What did they do in verse 12?

5) What are the details we learn in verses 13 through 43 about the Israelites? How many times did they disobey God?

6) Have you ever tried to earn someone's love? God's?

7) Read 1 Corinthians 13. What is love according to verses 4 through 7?

8) To someone who has never read this passage in 1 Corinthians, what does love look like?

9) Read James 2:14-26. What do you learn from these verses about faith and works?

10) Sometimes it is hard to accept the discipline of the Lord in our lives. Why do you think this is? What does Psalm 141:5 teach us?

#  Is for Mind

## God Says I Have the *Mind* of Christ

"For 'who has known the mind of the Lord that he may instruct Him?' But we have the *mind* of Christ."

1 Corinthians 2:16

*Mind*: intellect or understanding, as distinguished from the faculties of feeling and willing; intelligence (dictionary.com, 2011).

You probably have, at one time or another, read at least one children's book written by Dr. Seuss. I enjoy reading them to the little ones in my life these days. They are wonderful stories full of rhyme that really give me a good chuckle at times. He wrote so many great ones that it is hard to pick a favorite, but one I really love is *Oh the Thinks You Will Think*. It is a wonderful tale that encourages children to—you guessed it—think!

> You can think about red. You can think about pink. You can think up a horse. Oh the thinks you can think! Oh the thinks you can think up if only you try... Think left and think right and think low and think high, oh the thinks you can think up if only you try!

> Suess (1975)

It sure is a cute book for children, and we love to encourage children to use their imaginations, don't we? Whenever I heard those three little words every parent dreads, "I am bored," from one of my kids, my response was usually, "Well, use your imagination."

I love watching children use their imaginations. However, as adults sometimes the things that we "think up if only we try" may not be exactly the "thinks" that we should be thinking. Sometimes the private conversation I have inside my head is a conversation that I know should not be taking place. And while no one around me knows what I'm thinking, God always does, and He has a way of letting me know when my thoughts are not pleasing to Him. We have been given a warning as to what we should be doing with those types of conversations in 2 Corinthians 10:5. We are told to "take every thought captive to the obedience of Christ." The King James Bible puts it like this. "Casting down imaginations, and every high thing that exalteth itself against the knowledge of God, and bringing into captivity every thought to the obedience of Christ." As children we use our imagination for entertainment purposes, but as adults we must take control of our minds and not allow our imagination to run wild. Our mind can become a dangerous tool, which can be used to defeat us when we do.

I'm confident that I am not the only person who has allowed my imagination to get the best of me. I can imagine all sorts of things! There have been times when someone has walked by me and did not say hello or (supposedly) gave me a funny look. My initial assumption might be to think about what I did to make them mad at me. After our brother-in-law was killed in a car accident, if my husband was five minutes late pulling into the driveway from work, I would stand at the window, imagining the same tragedy happening to him. A physical symptom can make me imagine a deadly illness in a few days' time. A small argument with my husband can lead to a marriage crisis, ending with divorce and a division of property! I have a really good imagination, and if I do not guard my mind I can conceive all sorts of negativity. The thoughts that I allow to enter, if I am not careful, can easily consume me. Very quickly they can become crippling thoughts that want to keep me from living the life that God intended for me to live. That is why Paul told us to throw our imaginations right out the window and make sure we take them captive to the obedience of Christ.

In Greek the word "casting" is "*Kathaireo*," and it is defined as "to throw down, with the use of force." When the thoughts in our mind are not consistent with God's Word, we must throw them out with the use of force if necessary. That is a powerful thought, isn't it? I must become forceful in my thinking when my mind is being used for anything other than how God intended. I must take my thoughts captive, and I must do it on a regular basis. As soon as my mind begins to drift in the wrong direction it is essential that I spring into action to protect it.

Throughout history there have been many wars fought with the unfortunate result of many soldiers becoming prisoners of war. When someone is taken captive do you think the abductor does so by simply asking nicely, "Excuse me, would you please come with me? I am taking you captive now." Absolutely not! When you capture something it is usually done in a forceful manner. There is fight that goes into it, and it is done with the intent to not allow the prisoner to escape. That is exactly how we must protect our minds against the enemy who desires to take our thoughts captive. God's enemy is our enemy, and Satan knows that if we actually begin to think like Christ we will be powerful for God's Kingdom. My goodness! Can you imagine how your life could change if you only thought like Christ? We must be the ones to take every thought captive so all of our thoughts are obedient to Christ. That means making sure our minds are surrendered to Christ alone. We need to be careful that we do not set up park benches in our minds. We cannot afford to allow thoughts that enter to come in and sit on the park bench of our minds. You know how that goes, right? The thought is planted, and you mull it over and over and then over again. We allow it to fester, and pretty soon it is all we think about. When we do that, depression sets in, friendships die, unfaithfulness enters a marriage, suicide ends a life, churches become apathetic, and bitterness over our disappointments begin to rule our heart.

If we are going to cast down imaginations we must learn to discern between two things: our imagination and God's truth. Imagination is defined by dictionary.com as "the faculty of imagining, or of forming mental images or concepts of what is not actually present to the senses." In Greek the word imagination is "*logismos*," and it is defined as "a reckoning, reasoning such as is hostile to the Christian faith, a judgment or decision" (Strong's, Blue Letter Bible, 1996-2011). How do we know when our thoughts are hostile to the Christian faith? By knowing the truth about the Christian faith. We must know the Word of God. If we do not know what the Word says, or if we take the Word out of the context in which it was meant, we will not be able to discern between truth and error. We are told in 1 Corinthians 2:14 that "the natural man does not receive the things of the Spirit of God, for they are foolishness to him; nor can he know them, because they are spiritually discerned" (1 Corinthians 2:14). The natural man, who we are before we have accepted Christ as our Savior, does not have the Spirit of God living inside of him. The natural man cannot understand what a Christian believes or how he is to live. When a Christian states a truth from the Word of God, the natural man thinks it is foolish. We can see that in our society today, can't we? There are a few practices that are unacceptable to God; in fact, He calls them sins, but to the natural man they are completely acceptable (such as sex before marriage, cohabitating outside of marriage, homosexuality, stealing, adultery, lying, gossip, pride).

There have been times over the years when I have had to fight for my mind because of natural men. As I have grown in my walk

THE **ABC**'s OF WHO GOD SAYS I AM

with the Lord and my desire to serve Him has grown, the battle in my mind to believe the Word over what natural man might say about me has also grown. The more I learn about God and the more I understand about His ways, the less the natural man can understand me. This, at times, can be very hard when family and friends do not understand the changes in your life. People may not understand why you would not do the things you've always done with them and why certain practices aren't okay anymore. The stand for God you are taking now, that you never took before, makes no sense to those who do not know Christ. It seems like foolishness to them.

I will tell you honestly that as a people pleaser I have faced very difficult times in my life where I really thought I was going to lose my mind. I knew what the Word said, but I found myself surrounded by natural men who found my desire to serve the Lord completely foolish. Many times I was looked at like I had three heads when I would share from my heart the words of the Lord or a truth I found in the Bible. I had to overcome great fear of what others thought of me and I had to find my security in who God said I was and what God desired for me. Sometimes I would allow the fear of man, or the fear of being wrong, keep me from sharing what I knew the Word said. I was afraid of what men might think of me. I had to make a decision; whose approval was I going to live for? Once while in a place of confusion and fear, the Lord led me to this verse; "For God has not given us a spirit of fear, but of power and of love and of a sound mind" (2 Timothy 1:7). A sound mind? Not only can I have the mind of Christ, but I can have a sound mind, too! Hallelujah! The word *sound* in this verse in the Greek is "*sōphronismos*" and it is translated as, "an admonishing or calling to soundness of mind, to moderation and self-control" (Strongs, Blue Letter Bible, 1996-2011). I was amazed when I saw the word *self-control*. You mean I can control my thoughts? I do not need to live in fear nor be tormented in my mind because of the thoughts I have allowed to enter in? No,

I do not have to plant just any thought in the soil of my mind and allow it to grow there. It is up to me to determine what type of harvest I want to reap and then only allow that type of seed to be planted in my mind. We must learn to do the very thing God instructs us to do, and that is, "Cast down imaginations, and every high thing that exalts itself against the knowledge of God, and bring into captivity every thought to the obedience of Christ" (2 Corinthians 10:5).

Every minute of every day I am presented with three different opportunities where I can allow my mind to wander. I can choose to let it wander to the places that are pleasing to God, to the places Satan directs, or I can allow it to go to places that I take it. When I allow God control of my mind I am filled with thoughts that glorify Him, serve Him, and consider Him, His ways, and His Word. When my mind is on God, it is on His Word and truths that allow me to grow in my walk with Him. There is peace within me when I keep my thoughts focused on Him. There is a promise for us in Isaiah 26:3 that says, "You will keep him in perfect peace, whose mind is stayed on You, because he trusts in You." I can tell, you from a lady who was never at peace, that this verse is one you can take to the bank! The more Word I get into me, the more Word I focus on, and the more peaceful my life becomes. When I allow the circumstances of life and the trials I may walk through to take the forefront of my thoughts I can easily become a wreck. I get all flustered and irritated, and anxiety rises within me. When a situation is trying to consume my mind, I first must be willing to recognize what I am focused on. When the Lord shows me my focus is on the wrong thing, I quickly begin to speak the truth of God's word over that situation. The Word tells us that we *have the mind of Christ,* but as Christians we must *desire* to have the mind of Christ more than anything else. Romans 11:34 tells us that no one can comprehend all the ways of God. But through the guidance of the Holy Spirit, who is living in me, I can have spiritual insight into God's plans, His actions, and His ways of thinking. So how do we get the mind of Christ? Only through knowing the Word of God. As we study the Word and get it into our hearts, we must then begin to make the Word of God our confession. Speak the truth of God's Word out of your mouth, and you will see everything about your life change.

When we no longer listen to any voice but the Spirit speaking to us through the Word, we can begin to confess God's promises over the situations in life we are going through. Begin to memorize scripture, and when something creeps into your mind you know goes against the Word, you will have your weapon of the Word stashed away in your memory bank and can begin to speak it out. God told the Israelites to talk about Him. He wanted them to talk about His wondrous works. He wants that from us, too. He wants our speech to be about Him and all He has done, is doing, and will do. We could not and would not be able to do that with our mind continually focused on all our woes and troubles. Whatever we think about and focus on we talk about. If we truly want to understand what our minds should be set on so we can begin to think correctly, there is great instruction found in the book of Philippians. "Finally, my friends, keep your minds on whatever is true, pure, right, holy, friendly, and proper. Don't ever stop thinking about what is truly worthwhile and worthy of praise" (Philippians 4:8).

I say we begin to look for God in all situations and make *Him* the talk of the town—rather than the people of the town! We will come alive once our minds are set on all things worthwhile and worthy of praise. Don't you agree?

Questions to consider:

1) Can you relate to my stories on allowing my imagination to get the best of me? Do you have as good of an imagination as I do?

2) When you allow your mind to wander, where does it usually end up?

3) Have you ever been consumed by a thought that was not true, pure, right, holy, friendly, and proper?

4) Do you believe that you can have the mind of Christ?

5) Would you consider yourself to be a person with great self-control, moderate self-control, or little self-control?

6) When seeking advice, do you think it is important to talk to like-minded people? Why or why not? What can happen if you don't?

7) Have you ever had to take a strong stand for your beliefs? Do you do it forcefully, fearfully, or in confident faith?

8) How do you take your thoughts captive? How do you overcome wrong thoughts?

9) Have you ever allowed the fear of man to control you?

10) Spend some time this week asking the Lord to give you His mind and His way of thinking on every situation that comes your way. Write down any area that He shows your thoughts have been misguided or have been contrary to His Word.

# N Is for NEW

## God Says I am a *New* Creation

"Therefore, if anyone is in Christ, he is a *new* creation; old things have passed away; behold, all things have become new."

2 Corinthians 5:17

*New*: of a kind now existing or appearing for the first time; fresh or unused; other than the former (dictionary.com, 2011).

As I have been studying and contemplating these past few weeks on the word *new*, the Lord has drawn me to two very different creatures: caterpillars and the Apostle Paul. One is an insect that transforms into a beautiful butterfly, and the other is a strict Pharisee whom God transformed into an apostle who fully surrendered to Jesus Christ. I am awestruck by the radical changes that happened in the life of Paul. Just as a caterpillar sheds his skin (several times) and comes out of his cocoon a completely different being, Paul shed his Pharisee skin, went into the cocoon of separation from his old life, and became a completely different being, as well. I have loved getting to know Paul. Let's take a look at his story.

Paul was actually given the birth name of Saul, and he was born in Tarsus the son of a Pharisee from the tribe of Benjamin, raised in the strictest of Jewish homes. We learn in Acts 23:6 that he considered himself "a Pharisee, the son of a Pharisee." He studied with Gamaliel, one of the leading teachers of the time, who was greatly respected. In Acts 22:3 Paul stated, "I am a Jew, born in Tarsus of Cilicia, but brought up in this city. Under Gamaliel I was thoroughly trained in the law of our fathers and was just as zealous for God as any of you are today." Beth Moore writes in her book, *To Live Is Christ* , "His esteemed teacher was the rabbi Gamaliel, grandson of the great Hillel-names of great importance in the history of Judaism. So highly revered was Gamaliel that the Jews referred to him as 'the beauty of the law'" (Moore, To Live is Christ, 2001, p. 20)

Paul was a student of the law and he loved it. He studied it, and he knew it, and because of this he was determined to keep it. With his own words he said, "You know what I was like when I followed the Jewish religion—how I violently persecuted God's church. I did my best to destroy it. I was far ahead of my fellow Jews in my zeal for the traditions of my ancestors" (Galatians 1:13-14). Moore goes on to say,

> Obviously, Saul sat at the feet of one of Judaism's most grace-filled teachers; however, he soon developed his own ways of thinking. Saul's brilliance moved him to the front of every class. He was a born leader. You can be sure Saul rejoiced in taking a primary role in the endless debates on the interpretation of the law. The son of a Pharisee became a Pharisee.

> (Moore, To Live is Christ, 2001, p. 21)

Have you ever been so set in your ways that you could not see beyond it? There was no other way than your way? I know I have and I believe this to be exactly how Saul viewed the Jewish Law. It was the only way. *Who's Who in the Bible* states,

THE **ABC**'S OF WHO GOD SAYS I AM

Though Paul was probably in Jerusalem during the final period of Jesus's life, he never gives any hint in his writings that he saw or heard of Jesus during his ministry. It was only in later debates with Jesus's followers that Paul became alarmed at the rapid development of the movement...People like, Stephen, seemed determined to undermine the Law and worship at the holy temple, all in the name of Jesus of Nazareth (pg. 336).

Paul was just as determined to see this stopped. In his own words Paul goes on to say in Acts 22:4,

I persecuted the followers of this Way to their death, arresting both men and women and throwing them into prison, as also the high priest and all the Council can testify. I even obtained letters from them to their brothers in Damascus, and went there to bring these people as prisoners to Jerusalem to be punished.

Paul was there when Stephen, the first Christian to be martyred, was stoned.

And they cast him out of the city and stoned him. And the witnesses laid down their clothes at the feet of a young man named Saul. And they stoned Stephen as he was calling on God and saying, "Lord Jesus, receive my spirit."

Acts 7:58-59

Paul confessed in Acts 22:20 that he stood by, watching, consenting to Stephen's death. Can you see Saul's passion for his faith in the Law of God? He was raised in the law, he knew the law, and he was determined that all were going to follow that law. Saul was radical in his law-abiding ways, and in order for the

Lord to reach him He was going to have to reveal Himself in a radical sort of way. That is exactly what He did. Acts 9 tells the details of Paul's conversion on the road to Damascus.

> Meanwhile, Saul was still breathing out murderous threats against the Lord's disciples. He went to the high priest and asked him for letters to the synagogues in Damascus, so that if he found any there who belonged to the Way, whether men or women, he might take them as prisoners to Jerusalem. As he neared Damascus on his journey, suddenly a light from heaven flashed around him. He fell to the ground and heard a voice say to him, "Saul, Saul, why do you persecute me?" "Who are you, Lord?" Saul asked. "I am Jesus, whom you are persecuting," he replied. "Now get up and go into the city, and you will be told what you must do." The men traveling with Saul stood there speechless; they heard the sound but did not see anyone. Saul got up from the ground, but when he opened his eyes he could see nothing. So they led him by the hand into Damascus. For three days he was blind, and did not eat or drink anything.
>
> Acts 9:1-9

Three days blind and waiting. Can you imagine the thoughts that worked through his mind during those three days? Did he replay the scene over in his mind? Did he tell anyone that would listen, "I was just walking along the road when suddenly..." And all the while he sat waiting, another man, Ananias, was receiving his instructions to go to Saul and lay hands on him. I can understand why Ananias was a little concerned about this call of duty when he said, "Lord, I have heard many reports about this man and all the harm he has done to your saints in Jerusalem. And he has

come here with authority from the chief priests to arrest all who
call on your name" (Acts 9:13-14).

> But the Lord said to Ananias, "Go! This man is my chosen
> instrument to carry my name before the Gentiles and their
> kings and before the people of Israel." Then Ananias went
> to the house and entered it. Placing his hands on Saul,
> he said, "Brother Saul, the Lord—Jesus, who appeared to
> you on the road as you were coming here—has sent me so
> that you may see again and be filled with the Holy Spirit."
> Immediately, something like scales fell from Saul's eyes,
> and he could see again. He got up and was baptized, and
> after taking some food, he regained his strength.

> Acts 9:17-19

I love the declaration that God made to Ananias when he told
him that Saul was "His chosen instrument to carry His name to
the Gentiles." God had a plan and purpose for Saul his entire
life. Nothing in Saul's life would be wasted just like nothing in
our lives is ever wasted unless we refuse to allow God access to
it to use it for His purposes and glory. I once heard a statement
that God would not protect us from anything that He can use
to perfect us. Something like scales fell from Saul's eyes, and he
could see again. Only this time he saw the truth. He saw Jesus
for who Jesus really was—the Son of God. He saw His life with a
new purpose, a new call, and a new passion. He wasted absolutely
no time as the Word goes on to say, "At once he began to preach
in the synagogues that Jesus is the Son of God" (Acts 9:21). What
an incredible example of old things passing away and all things
becoming new. He became a new man with a new name. He
changed from Saul defender of the law to Paul defender of Jesus.

Now, you may be wondering what Paul and caterpillars
have in common. Transformation. After a little research I have

discovered that between five and ten days after a butterfly lays her eggs they hatch. Ehow.com describes what happens next. "These tiny creatures are ravenous and quickly begin to eat away at every leaf in sight. During this time of tremendous growth, the caterpillar sheds its skin several times, becoming stronger and larger with each turn." (Simmons, 1999-2011)

I can relate to this little caterpillar. Like Paul I had to have scales removed from my eyes so I could see the real Jesus. When they fell I was a hungry, hungry girl! I wanted to know all I could know of Him, and I began to devour His Word. I "ate" everything I could to gain more knowledge. I listened to teachings, I read the Bible and studied books, and I became consumed by the desire to know more. This was the beginning process of my new life in Christ. By getting into the Word and discovering all I could about God and His Ways I also began to shed some old skin, some old ways of thinking, and some old habits and attitudes that weren't very pleasing or glorifying to God. Oh friend, let us not hold onto our old way of thinking for too long; we just might be a Saul—sincere but sincerely wrong.

The next step for the caterpillar is the cocoon stage. All the changes the caterpillar goes through are done in private. The entire structure of a caterpillar is being changed into something completely different. A butterfly is forming. From the inside of its chrysalis where no one can see, miraculous things are happening. That is exactly how God begins the changes in each one of us—from within the privacy of our own hearts and minds. Once we begin to know and understand His Word we cannot help but change. We are reminded again that He renews our minds. Romans 12:2 says, "Don't copy the behavior and customs of this world, but let God transform you into a new person by changing the way you think. Then you will learn to know God's will for you, which is good and pleasing and perfect" (Romans 12:2). Amazing changes occur in us when we hold nothing back from God and we learn to submit to His plan. He longs for us to allow Him to work within us in an intimate way. Paul spent some time in his own cocoon, beginning with the days he was blind. I can only imagine what went on inside his heart and mind as he sat there waiting. But when his sight was restored he got up and never went back to his old way of life. The butterfly does not go back to a caterpillar; it stays a butterfly. That's where many of us lose out. We think our past disqualifies us for a future with God. Paul did not allow his past to disqualify him; he used it as part of his testimony for God. He wasn't afraid to tell everyone, "This is what I was, and now this is who I am." We might have a great conversion experience and be ready to go with God, but fear stops us. Or we may go to church and read the Word, but we never fully surrender to the truth of it. We never allow the new life to begin. We hold onto the past, thinking we are too sinful for God to fully forgive. Or we slip back into an old habit, and while we know it is not pleasing to God we surrender to the habit instead of Him. Or we just refuse to allow God access to our entire heart. Maybe we just like our sin too much to let it go because it is more comfortable to hold on to it than release it.

"New butterflies will spend time beating their wings, acclimating themselves and growing stronger. As the wings beat, their circulatory systems fill and the butterfly becomes viable" (Simmons, 1999-2011). As a new creation in Christ we need to beat our wings, acclimate ourselves, and grow stronger, too. It says that as the butterfly beats its wings their circulatory systems fill, and they become viable. Viable means capable of living! The word *beat* is defined this way, "to strike violently or forcefully and repeatedly" (dictionary.com, 2011). The butterfly knows that it has to beat its wings in order to live. We beat our wings when we fight against the wicked schemes of the devil, who desires to keep us bound to our old ways of thinking and living. We beat our wings because we will not allow anything to stand between us and God. We know without a doubt that we are viable only when completely surrendered to Him. We beat our wings when we become determined to read the Word each day and obey it. We beat our wings when we decide we want to grow and mature in God's ways. As a butterfly beats its wings, its circulatory system fills—just as we beat ours by doing whatever is necessary to live for Christ. We are filled with the Holy Spirit of God and a new way of living has begun. We can let the old pass away and no longer be in bondage to it. What a miracle!

There is a time, however, where danger lurks for the butterfly. The website goes on to say, "During this time they are easy prey, because they have no defenses and are unable to fly" (Simmons, 1999-2011). We must remember that although we have a new life in Christ, there are times when our defenses are down; we might be weak and become easy prey. Some of my greatest hurts in life have come through the hands, mouths, and attitudes of friends and family who couldn't accept the new things God was doing inside of me. Paul had to let go of his entire life, as he had known it, once he gave his life to Christ. I wonder what Paul's friends and fellow Pharisee students thought of his sudden transformation. The Old Saul as they once knew him—known for approving the killing of Christ followers was now one of them. It cost Paul a great deal to live for Christ, and it will cost us, too. As God makes changes on the inside, and those changes seep to the outside others will begin to notice them. Some will accept the changes, and some may not. God may decide to remove people from our lives who do not allow the butterfly to fly. Although it might be extremely painful to let go and move on with God, good always comes from walking in His plans.

I believe one area we must become better at living, within the body of believers, is in encouraging other Christians in the process of change. I have seen other Christians reject and ridicule growth in fellow believers, and I have often wondered why. What is it that keeps us from rejoicing with others when God moves within their lives? Is it jealousy, competition, our own insecurities? We must be careful that we do not stunt another believer's growth. We are called as believers to "encourage one another daily" (Hebrews 3:12-14). We must begin to point out the good things we see in one another, not the bad. We always bring it up and remind each other what we were, or still are, in "our opinion." God is always doing a new thing. Often we only see things through our flesh and never take the time to ask God what He is doing and how He is moving, so when changes begin, fear takes over instead of trust. When that happens we try to hold on to what was, and we never grow. We must not fear those changes and allow God to do the new work. Let's allow one another the opportunity to change and encourage each other as we walk through those changes. Change can be very hard, and we need one another's support during those times.

God has so much in store for each one of us in the new life He has planned for us. We must become hungry for the Word, shed some skin, and go into the cocoon for a season of intimacy. Then we will beat our wings, acclimate ourselves, and become stronger. We must be careful we do not become easy prey for the enemy.

Oh, beautiful butterfly, spread your wings and fly. Live in the new life Christ has for you. Do not be afraid of it and embrace all He has for you!

Questions to consider:

1) Have you ever been tricked into believing that somehow your mistakes disqualify you from being used by God?

2) Many times in the Bible God changed people's names at a turning point in their life. Jacob became Israel, Saul became Paul, Abram became Abraham, and Simon became Peter. When was your turning point with the Lord?

3) What new name might God give to you?

4) What area(s) of your life have you seen God make a change in? Could it be it is an old behavior, attitude, mind-set, addiction or_____?

5) Can you recognize any area(s) in your life God wants to bring new life to?

6) Sometimes change can seem overwhelming. Where does Psalm 61:2 tell us to go when we are overwhelmed?

7) The changes in you should make those around you think, but it shouldn't scare them away. How can we keep this in balance?

8) Read Hebrews 3:12-13 and 10:23-25. What are we to do according to these verses?

9) Do you have any fear about allowing God to make the changes in you *as He sees fit*? If so, what are they?

10) God desires for us to let go of the flesh and live according to the Spirit. Read Galatians 5:19-26. List the works of the flesh and then the Fruits of the Spirit.

# O IS FOR OVERCOME

## God Says I Have Overcome

"And they *overcame* him by the blood of the Lamb and by the word of their testimony, and they did not love their lives to the death."

Revelation 12:11

*Overcome:* to get the better of in a struggle or conflict; conquer; defeat: to prevail over (dictionary.com).

We've just worked through the letter M, which told us we had the *mind* of Christ, and the letter N, which told us we were *new* in Christ. Next I believe we need to take the letter O and talk about overcoming the battles that want to keep us locked in our old ways of thinking and living. The word *overcome* in the original Greek is the word *nikaō,* which means; to conquer, to carry off the victory, come off victorious; of Christ, victorious over all His foes; "of Christians, that hold fast their faith even unto death against the power of their foes, and temptations and persecutions; or when one is arraigned or goes to law, to win the case, maintain one's cause" (Strongs, Blue Letter Bible- Lexicon, 1996-2011). Jesus had a very important message to share with his disciples in John 16:33 when He said,

notice that there are many people who are choosing to walk on the lower, wide path, and they seem to know what they are doing. The Guide to the upper path assures you that the view from this path is the one you want to see. As those who are walking on the upper narrow path begin their journey, they discover that they have a lot to overcome to get up to this path. This mountain is steep, and to reach the upper path there is a hard climb involved. Many have brought excessive baggage with them that they thought they might need along the way. They soon learn that they are going to have to let that go if they want to reach the narrow path. The climb is too steep to try and hold unnecessary items. The Guide knows what you will need and what you can let go of. You can trust Him to release what He tells you to. Some decide it is too hard to relinquish their items that they've brought along, so they turn and decide to walk the wide path.

You weigh your options and decide to take the lower path while others make the decision to walk on the upper path. You begin your journey. Soon you discover, however, that this path does not look quite like you thought it did from the gate. As you walk around the side of the path it begins to dip down very low and becomes fog covered. There are many roots from the trees in the path, and it is not maintained very well. As you trip over obstacles, stumble through traps, and fall repeatedly, you realize that this path is much more challenging to walk on than first expected. Yet in the beginning, it seemed to be the easiest route. The dense fog makes it difficult to see. You must just follow those walking with you, guessing at what steps you should take next. The view that looked so pretty at the gate has quickly become very dark and gray. Hope soon turns to hopelessness as you feel your way along this path. Fear sets in as there seems to be no way off this path or out of this situation. Along the way you pick up baggage others from the upper path have dropped, thinking you might need to hold on to it for later use.

You believed that there would be less pain involved if you took the lower path because it did not appear as hard to get to as the upper path. And there seemed to be less effort involved. You reasoned with yourself that though it may take you longer to get to the top of the mountain from the lower path, you knew that eventually you'd get there. But now the guide that you thought was there to help you along this path has shown his true colors; he's a deceiver. He has left everyone to fend for themselves. He is really just enjoying the show. He delights in watching everyone struggle along the path. It is very humorous to him. You discover he is no help at all. His only desire is to watch everyone stumble and fall and become frustrated, angry, confused, insecure, and disheartened. He loves to see resentment build in the hearts of those on the lower path. Jealousy consumes them as they hear the voices of those who have chosen the other path as they sing songs of joy and freedom. His true intentions were to keep everyone from the upper path and that *other* Guide. He cannot stand that other Guide; there's a lot of jealousy there. The lower guide wanted the upper path to call his own and thought he could overtake the Guide on that path. He was wrong and was told he would have to stay on this lower path now. His plan now is to keep people from walking on the upper path with the Guide he despises so much. Every so often there is a path that leads to the upper path, but he is going to fight every attempt you make to leave his path. He loves to watch lost people fail in their efforts to find their way off of the lower path. Through trickery and deception he will make you think there is no way out. The Word says in Matthew 7:13-14,

> You can enter God's Kingdom only through the narrow gate. The highway to hell is broad, and its gate is wide for the many who choose that way. But the gateway to life is very narrow and the road is difficult, and only a few ever find it.
>
> Matthew 7:13-14

Satan is hoping we never find that narrow path, but if we do notice it, he is scheming to prevent us from walking on it. If we begin to walk on the narrow path, he hopes we will grow weary of it and want to get off. If he can convince us the path is too narrow and difficult to follow, then he's kicking his heels in celebration.

Satan is also the "accuser of the brethren who stands before God and accuses night and day" (Revelation12:10). Every time you or I slip up, he's right there to point out our transgression to the Father. That's why we need the blood of Christ. The blood Jesus shed covered all of our sins, and when Satan accuses us, Jesus stands up and says, "That sin has been covered by My blood, Father." That's one of the ways we overcome Satan according to Revelation 12:11, by the blood of the Lamb. Jesus's blood became the atoning sacrifice needed to overcome our sin debt we couldn't pay. So when Satan accuses or brings back to memory a sin that you've repented for, just remind him (and yourself) that that sin has been washed clean by the blood of the Lamb.

The verse in Revelation 12 goes on to say that we also overcome Satan by the Word of our testimony. The word is *Logos*, the spoken Word of God. We overcome Satan by speaking the Word of God as a testimony to what God has done in our lives. As Christians, we can choose to allow the world and all its suffering to overcome us, or we can overcome the world by the power of the Word. If we want to be overcome by the world then we speak negative, hopeless, fearful statements. We can voice our problems continuously and focus solely on them. But we can overcome the trials and tribulations that we face in the world by looking into the Word and finding our promises and giving testimony to them. Speak the Word of God over the situation. How can we identify the truth when we are in the middle of a situation? The Word is always the safest place to go when searching for truth. It is the only Truth. While reading Psalm 119, I found many answers to areas that I've struggled to overcome in my own life. Here are some ways we can overcome Satan's schemes. First begin to seek God with your whole heart. Always seeking God with your whole heart is one way to keep you on the path He has for you. Know His laws and follow them. You may be wondering how you can live a pure life. The Word in verse nine of Psalm 119 tells us it is by living according to God's Word. How can we recognize sin? Put God's Word in your heart. Verse 11 says, "I have hidden Your word in my heart that I might not sin against You." How do we overcome the lie that makes us think we could not understand God's Word? Pray verse 18 each time you open your bible, "Open my eyes that I may see wonderful things in Your law." Where can we find good counsel when we need it? "Your statutes are my delight; they are my counselors" (verse 24). How can I overcome lying? Pray this way, "Remove from me the way of lying, and grant me Your law graciously." Then speak this out loud, "I have chosen the way of truth; Your judgments I have laid before me" (verses 29 and 30). God can help us make good decisions for our lives when we cry out to Him. "Teach me knowledge and good judgment, for I believe in your commands."

There are so many more verses in Psalm 119. I encourage you to read through and discover which ones the Lord has chosen specifically for you. How do we follow that narrow path that Matthew 7 talks about? The Message Bible puts Psalm 119:1 this way:

> You're blessed when you stay on course, walking steadily on the road revealed by God. You're blessed when you follow his directions, doing your best to find him. That's right—you don't go off on your own; you walk straight along the road he set.

As we seek to overcome the world and all the bad habits we pick up from living in this world, let this be our prayer.

Barricade the road that goes Nowhere; grace me with your clear revelation. I choose the true road to Somewhere; I post your road signs at every curve and corner. I grasp and cling to whatever you tell me; God, don't let me down! I'll run the course you lay out for me if you'll just show me how.

Psalms 119:25b (The Message).

Questions to consider:

1) List your understanding of Satan and his ways and then read Isaiah 14:12-21 and explain what took place.

2) What happened in Matthew 4 between Jesus and Satan?

3) Read Luke 22:2-4. What happened to Judas? Why?

4) What does 2 Corinthians 11:14 tell us about Satan?

5) Who did Paul say hindered them in 1 Thessalonians 2:18?

6) Should Satan be blamed for everything that goes wrong in our lives? Read 1 Peter 5: 5-11. What can we learn from these verses?

7) What does Revelation 12:9 tell Satan does?

8) What is the Word to us according to Psalm 119:105?

9) What do we learn from reading Ephesians 6:10-20?

10) What does Psalm 119:101 say?

# P IS FOR PURPOSE

## God Says He Has a Purpose for My Life

"The Lord will fulfill His *purpose* for me; Your love, O Lord, endures forever—do not abandon the works of Your hands."

Psalm 138:8

*Purpose*: the reason for which something exists or is done, made, used, etc. (dictionary.com).

I am a planner. I like to have a plan. And because I am a planner I have a family of planners. I think it may even drive our beautiful daughter-in-law a bit on the crazy side with all our planning. In September I want to know what we are doing for Thanksgiving. In October, Christmas plans need to be ironed out. Yes, I like to have a plan. I work best that way. So you might think that having eighteen years to plan for the day we would become empty nesters would be enough time for me. But when our youngest son graduated from high school, and I stepped into a new season of life to which I did not have a plan, I began to become a little distressed. Throughout the years I was at home doing the "mommy" job. I had some ideas of what I *thought* I would be doing as this season approached, but when the day finally arrived not one of those dreams had become a reality. Truthfully, I had some pretty grandiose plans for myself. So when I was now an empty nester without any of my plans being fulfilled, I can honestly say I was not prepared for the extent of emotion that I would have to work through. I began to wonder where I fit. I really began to lose sight of having any purpose or any direction. This became a time when asking the Lord to reveal to me the purpose for my life was forefront in my heart. I needed to know that He had a plan for me and that He hadn't forgotten about me because, honestly, I thought He had. I thought I knew exactly what God had prepared for me, but it seemed that every attempt I made to move towards my dream, led to a dead-end road. I began to wait, and I began to study, and I began to seek. Then I began to discover, and I began to change.

One discovery I made was the need I had to *be* someone. I wanted my life to *mean* something. I really wanted to know that my life had a *purpose*. And now as I have traveled along my journey I have found that deep inside each of us there is a similar longing. We all have a longing for purpose. We want to know that we have a reason for existing. As I think back to my growing up years, I recognize now that I never stopped and said, "I wonder what God put me here for," or, "I wonder what God's purpose for my life is." Not once. To be honest, I did not spend a lot of time in my teen years thinking about God. While this brings some sadness to my heart, it also brings thankfulness because I am proof that it is never too late to ask Him to use us for His purpose. What I discovered in my time of seeking is that we all want our lives to have purpose, but we will search and search until we discover that our real reason for existing is *for Him*. We were created *by* Him, *for* Him.

"For by Him all things were created: things in heaven and on earth, visible and invisible, whether thrones or powers or rulers or authorities; all things were created by Him and for Him" (Colossian 1:16).

In 2002 Pastor Rick Warren wrote a devotional book called *The Purpose Driven Life*. If you want to read a book that inspires you to find your true purpose in Christ, you must read this one. He begins the very first chapter with this statement:

> It is not about you. The purpose of your life is far greater than your own personal fulfillment, your peace of mind, or even your happiness. It is far greater than your family, your career, or even your wildest dreams and ambitions. If you want to know why you were placed on this planet, you must begin with God. You were born *by* His purpose and *for* His purpose (Warren, 2002).

I never even considered that I was born by His purpose and for His purpose. In fact, I do not remembering hearing that once during my weekly visits to Sunday school. It has taken me many years to figure this out! What transforming revelation it was when it finally clicked inside my heart that God made me *for* Him and knows the plan and purpose He has for my life! I was seeking ways to find fulfillment and purpose for myself to make *me* happy. I began to realize that He does have a plan for my life and a big part of that is to make sure I do everything for His glory. He speaks through Jeremiah in Jeremiah 29:11 and says, "For I know the plans I have for you... plans to prosper you and not to harm you, plans to give you hope and a future" (Jeremiah 29:11). His plan for each of us is full of hope and prosperity. But there are days when we might find it difficult to hold onto that statement. Throughout our lifetimes we will have experiences that are great and some not so great. In fact, some can be so devastating that it may seem difficult to even function. But God is so faithful that He can use the most painful trials we go through. The occasions that can cause the most damage within our hearts, the events that we could not possibly believe anything good could come from, He knows that He can bring something good out of them if we will allow Him. We find this promise in Romans 8:28.

"We are assured and know that [God being a partner in their labor] all things work together and are [fitting into a plan] for good to and for those who love God and are called according to [His] design and purpose" (Romans 8:28).

Notice that this verse is about allowing ourselves to rely on the knowledge that He can work all things together for good and that they are "fitting into a plan." We may not always know what the plan is right away or even like the idea that this is part of a plan, but God is always a Good God, and He can be trusted to help us in our times of need.

Often in death or illness we question God's purpose. When we experience the death of a loved one we wonder why God let them die. We hear the stories of young children with cancer or other diseases and wonder why God allows suffering or death of the young and innocent. When tragedy hits us our first thoughts aren't usually, *What good can you bring out of this situation, Lord?* But I truly believe that is exactly what He desires from us. We must fight the urge to blame God and instead seek Him diligently to find our comfort, our hope, and our purpose in the situation we are walking through. We need to ask, "How can I help others see God in this? How can God be glorified in this situation? How can God use me in this? How can God overcome evil with good during this time?"

A few months after our son graduated and moved out of the house one of our best friends was killed in an automobile accident. It was as though the earth stopped turning for us. We had planned and dreamed about the future with this couple and what God was going to do with our lives together. And then one day we got a phone call that his life was no longer here. Once again I felt as though I was struggling to understand my purpose and my place and what purpose there was for this tragic loss. I began to ask the Lord over and over, "Show me where I can find you in this situation, Lord. It hurts and I am full of pain and sorrow, but I want to see Your glory in it." He said,

"Call to Me and I will answer you and show you great and mighty things, fenced in and hidden, which you do not know [do not distinguish and recognize, have knowledge of and understand]" (Jeremiah 33:3, Amplified Bible).

Call out to Him in your pain and sorrow. He wants to answer you.

If we acknowledge that we were created *by* God *for* God, we would recognize that we can not trust in ourselves or our own abilities to obtain purpose. We will only be content with our purpose in a life surrendered to Christ. When we allow ourselves to believe our purpose depends solely on our abilities and accomplishments, we run the risk of suffering great disappointment. I have been a witness to lives that have allowed tragic accidents to prevent individuals from believing they have any purpose in life because they believed purpose was found in their own abilities. Rather than believing they were created *by* God *for* God, their lives overflowed with despair and defeat. They now have hearts full of bitterness over what was lost. An accident stole from them more than just dreams of the future; it also stole all passion for life. Rather than seeking God and allowing Him to use them for His glory, they only see what they have lost. I recently saw Joni Eareckson Tada speak on *Larry King Live*. Her testimony spoke loudly of where and *in Whom* she found her purpose. She was injured in a diving accident in 1967 that left her a quadriplegic and unable to use her hands or legs. In the interview, she spoke of depression and discouragement along with her desire to commit suicide. Then she shared how she began to pray, "God, if I could not die, please show me how to live." We may not all lose the use of our arms and legs, but we all suffer loss in our lives at one time or another. Wouldn't it be wonderful if we all began to pray that prayer now, "God show me how to live"? I found her written testimony on her website:

> I am convinced that God's motive, God's purpose, His plan in the accident in which I became paralyzed, His purpose was to turn a head strong stubborn rebellious

kid into a young woman who would reflect something of patience, something of endurance, something of long suffering. Who would get her life values turned from wrong side down to right side up and would have a buoyant and lively optimistic hope of heavenly glories above (Joniearecksontadastory.com).

God's purpose was far different in her life than I am sure she had planned for herself. She was a teenager enjoying a hot summer day, getting ready to go off to college, when suddenly her life was forever changed. If Joni had been able to use her arms, she might have never found enjoyment with the paintings she created with her mouth. There would not be a ministry called "Joni and Friends," which is dedicated to people with disabilities and their families. She has allowed God to *turn all things together for good* because she found purpose beyond her physical abilities. She was able to look to the Master Creator, the Creator of the universe, and trust that He still had a purpose for her life. She lives out each day for Him, not herself. God has made each one of us with His own hand and we were made for His glory, not ours. Isaiah 43:7 reminds us, "Everyone who is called by my name, whom I have created for my glory; I have formed him, yes, I have made him" (Isaiah 43:7).

I do not believe it is necessary to experience a tragedy like Joni did to make us question our life's purpose. We all do it from time to time. We contemplate what we should be doing now that we have our college education. Or like me we wonder what we should do now that the kids have all moved out of the house. If we're not careful selfishness and pride can very easily become the driving force behind our desire to find purpose. If I leave God out and allow my focus to be solely on what I *feel* my purpose is or what I *want* my purpose to be in life, I can very easily become self-centered and self-serving. And then what happens if I do not fulfill the purpose I believe I am supposed to fulfill? What happens if I believe my purpose is to be a great wife and my marriage ends in divorce? Did I fulfill my purpose? If I find my life's purpose in being a devoted mother to my children, what happens when my children leave home and I encounter the empty nest? What happens if I decide that my purpose is to be a singer that is known across the world yet I never obtain that dream? If I find my purpose in making a lot of money, what happens if I lose my job or go bankrupt? Where will I find my purpose if I've been looking for it in things? If I do not have the *things* I've been seeking all along, what then? Proverbs 11:28 from the Message says it best this way, "Our purpose is not to make a lot of money- A life devoted to things is a dead life, a stump; a God-shaped life is a flourishing tree." If I am just living each day trying to obtain my purpose without the understanding that I was created *by* God *for* God, my life is going to be empty.

When I look within the Word I can and will find His promises, instructions, and His desires for me. Through His Word I know that one of His purposes for my life is to do good works for Him. "For we are His workmanship, created in Christ Jesus for good works, which God prepared beforehand that we should walk in them" (Ephesians 2:10). I love this verse from the Message Bible:

> It is in Christ that we find out who we are and what we are living for. Long before we first heard of Christ and got our hopes up, He had His eye on us, had designs on us for glorious living, part of the overall purpose He is working out in everything and everyone.
>
> Ephesians 1:11-12.

We do not have to live our lives in a state of despair and depression. Glorious living does not mean dreading each morning when the alarm goes off and feeling like we just could not face another day because we do not find any purpose in the days we live. Living a gratifying and noble life filled with purpose is the kind of life God wants us to live. When we stop trying to decide what our purpose in life is and ask Him to help us find our purpose in Him, we will. You may be in a job that you just do not enjoy. Every day is a battle just to get enough energy to go. The people are miserable to be around, and there is little joy in being there. Rather than focus on the negative aspects of it, as difficult as that may be, instead begin to ask God to show you His purpose for you being there. God does place us in positions to accomplish His works. Could it be, possibly, that there is a coworker caught in a sin who the Lord wants you to befriend and share His love with? Might there be a friend at the end of their rope who needs to hear the wonderful salvation message of Christ? It is not always easy to look beyond our own emotions in a situation that is tough, but that is what God is asking us to do. Lay down your emotions and what you think and feel with your flesh and look to Him to show you His purpose. Then follow His directions as He leads you to walk in them.

We must look to Jesus as our example. He lived to die. He was sent by the Father to speak for Him and be a Witness for Him. In John 8:28 He said He did nothing on His own. "So Jesus said, 'When you have lifted up the Son of Man, then you will know that I am the one I claim to be and that I do nothing on My own but speak just what the Father has taught Me'" (John 8:28). His purpose was to come and lead people to the Father through His sacrifice on the cross for our sins. Maybe it is time that we followed His example by living our lives speaking only that which we have learned from Him. We must have our eyes fixed on knowing that He has a far greater purpose for our lives than we could ever think or imagine.

Life is full of changes, and God calls them "seasons." Ecclesiastes 3:1-8 reminds us that there is a time for everything.

> To everything there is a season, A time for every purpose under heaven: A time to be born, And a time to die; A

time to plant, And a time to pluck what is planted; A time to kill, And a time to heal; A time to break down, And a time to build up; A time to weep, And a time to laugh; A time to mourn, And a time to dance; A time to cast away stones, And a time to gather stones; A time to embrace, And a time to refrain from embracing; A time to gain, And a time to lose A time to keep, And a time to throw away; A time to tear, And a time to sew; A time to keep silence, And a time to speak; A time to love, And a time to hate, A time of war, And a time of peace.

Ecclesiastes 3:1-8

There is a time for every purpose under heaven. As seasons change in our lives and people come and go, we must remember to never hold on to things too tightly. God's on the move, and if we are to fulfill all the purposes He has for us we must be ready to move with Him.

There are going to be many times in our lives when we will have the opportunity to question, wonder, and doubt but we must always keep ourselves connected to God during those times. Stay in the Word and do not run from it. Continue to be in fellowship with other believers and remain faithful in attending church. God has a purpose for each one of us, and the trials and tests we go through in life can be used to glorify Him in our testimony. I've heard it said our mess can be our message and our test can be our testimony. We must make sure we plant our feet on Christ the Solid Rock.

Questions to consider:

1) Helen Keller said, "Many people have a wrong idea of what constitutes true happiness. It is not attained

through self-gratification, but through fidelity to a worthy purpose." What's your idea of true happiness?

2) What does Psalm 119:73 say?

3) Have you experienced a tragedy in your life that made you question God's goodness?

4) In your suffering was/is anger, bitterness and resentment an option for you? How do/will you protect your heart from these emotions?

5) Too often these days we are living just for the day. Just for the pleasure of that moment. We are looking for the feeling of purpose. How do we overcome the pull of finding purpose in things other than God?

6) Do you believe, and trust, that you were created *by* God, *for* God, for His purposes for your life?

7) Romans 5:8 tells us the extent of God's love. What does it say?

8) God used many people in the Bible for His purposes. Is there someone you have read about that you admire for allowing God to use them? Explain who and why.

9) Did you have big hopes and dreams as a child? Did you fulfill them? Do you see God in any of them?

10) Do you believe that God knows the plans He has for you and that they are full of hope and a desire to prosper you? Read 3 John 1:2, what does it say?

# Q Is for Qualified

## God Says I Am Qualified

"Giving thanks to the Father, Who has *qualified* and made us fit to share the portion which is the inheritance of the saints (God's holy people) in the Light."

Colossians 1:12

*Qualified*: having the qualities, accomplishments, etc., that fit a person for some function, office, or the like (dictionary.com, 2011).

Not too long ago we met a couple from the church we were attending and became good friends with them. The husband is a lawyer and owns his own practice. One day his wife told me that he had something he wanted to talk to me about, and I was surprised when he offered me a job working in his office. I had worked as a secretary once before but never for a lawyer. I was astonished at the offer since I had absolutely no paralegal training. When I told him that, he simply said, "That's okay. I will teach you, and you can be trained in all that you need to know." He saw something in me that he thought he could work with, and he had a need in his office for a secretary. He knew that I was going to need a lot of time to learn and that I was going to make mistakes along the way. He also realized that it was going to take some time before I understood all there was to know about the job and the law, in particular. With no qualification at all for the job, he was willing to look beyond all that I lacked and look instead at the potential I had. I believe that is exactly how God works with us. He looks beyond what we perceive as our lack and looks instead to what He knows is our potential. He knows that He has qualified us to do the work He has set before us.

This scripture and this word *qualified* have made me think a lot about the "saints in the light" the verse mentions. It has made me stop to consider how qualified the men and women before us were that God used so mightily. What made the twelve disciples qualified to be the twelve disciples? What did Jesus see in these men that made Him call each of them to come and follow Him? He saw two fishermen, brothers Simon Peter and Andrew. There was James the son of Zebedee and his brother John, also fishermen. Matthew was a tax collector, and Simon was called a Zealot, which is a nice word for fanatic. Jesus even chose Judas Iscariot, the one who would betray him. Is that what qualified him to be chosen? Jesus needed someone who would be willing to betray Him, and He knew Judas would do it. I think about the Old Testament heroes of the Bible—Noah, Abraham, Isaac, Jacob, Joseph, Moses, David, Sarah, and others— who were men and woman God chose and used for His specific purpose. Oh, how I would have loved to be with those who have gone before me and learned from them. Would you have loved to be a fly on the wall with these great servants of God? Their stories are full of awe and wonder that show the greatness of God in the lives of ordinary people whom God chose to use in extraordinary ways.

I began to wonder what qualifications the older heroes had for the job titles God gave them. Noah built an ark, yet I do not find in the Bible that he was a master craftsman. Moses was chosen to lead God's people out of Egypt, yet he felt inadequate because of a speech impediment (Exodus 4:10). In fact, when God came to Moses and introduced Himself in the burning bush, Moses asked Him, "Who am I that I should go?" I noticed that God did not give him the list of his qualifications. He just told him that He would be with him and He showed Moses three signs to prove it. God called Abraham out from his father's home to a land that He would show him. Then He made a covenant with him that he would make him into a great nation (Genesis 12.1-3). David was taken from a shepherd in the pasture to shepherding God's people. He promised David that His Kingdom would last forever (2 Samuel 7:16). We can see that God picked these men and used them, but I wonder what it was about them; what did they have in common? Then I discovered something in Hebrews 11, a little word with a powerful punch called Faith. Hebrews 11 is called "The Faith Chapter," and it begins this way. "Now faith is the assurance (the confirmation, the title deed) of the things [we] hope for, being the proof of things [we] do not see and the conviction of their reality [faith perceiving as real fact what is not revealed to the senses" (Hebrews 11:1, Amplified Bible).

I saw the thread that tied all of the men and woman of the Bible together with God; it was the thread of faith. Faith ties them all together, and faith can tie me to them!

"For by [faith-trust and holy fervor born of faith] the men of old had divine testimony borne to them and obtained a good report" (Hebrews 11:2, Amplified Bible). Holy fervor is living with a dedicated passion. Their lives were lived with dedicated passion for the Lord.

Here's what we can learn about Noah from this chapter:

[Prompted] by faith Noah, being forewarned by God concerning events of which as yet there was no visible sign, took heed and diligently and reverently constructed and prepared an ark for the deliverance of his own family. By this [his faith which relied on God] he passed judgment and sentence on the world's unbelief and became an heir and possessor of righteousness (that relation of being right into which God puts the person who has faith).

Hebrews 1:7

We read this about Abraham:

> [Urged on] by faith Abraham, when he was called, obeyed
> and went forth to a place which he was destined to receive
> as an inheritance; and he went, although he did not know
> or trouble his mind about where he was to go. [Prompted]
> by faith he dwelt as a temporary resident in the land which
> was designated in the promise [of God, though he was like
> a stranger] in a strange country, living in tents with Isaac
> and Jacob, fellow heirs with him of the same promise.

Hebrews 1:8-9 (Amplified Bible)

For Sarah, the wife of Abraham, it is written:

> Because of faith also Sarah herself received physical power
> to conceive a child, even when she was long past the age for
> it, because she considered [God] Who had given her the
> promise to be reliable and trustworthy and true to His Word.

Hebrews 1:11 (Amplified Bible)

What a faith builder Hebrews 11 is for us! As I read through the
chapter and saw each of the names, I realized that it was *by faith*
that God qualified them. As we look at the disciples that Jesus
called to be "fishers of men" we see that they were men whom we
view as men of great faith. But do you realize that those who had
great faith also had times of great struggle? Abraham and Sarah lied
not once but twice about their marital status (Genesis 12 & 20).
Sarah actually laughed when she first heard that she would bear a
child in her old age (Genesis18:12). Moses killed a man (Exodus
2:12). David slept with a woman who was not his wife and then had
her husband killed (2 Samuel 11). As a teen Joseph seemed to have
a bit of pride and be something of a tattletale, which provoked his

brother's hatred of him (Genesis 37). Peter rebuked Jesus to whom Jesus replied, "Get behind Me, Satan!" (Matthew 16:22-23), and He also denied Jesus three times. In fact, all but one of the disciples abandoned Jesus at the cross (Matthew 26). And we already know that Judas betrayed Jesus for thirty pieces of silver.

I have often questioned my abilities and my rights as a Christian as I wonder how He could use me for His glory. How could I be qualified to carry His message of hope to those whom He brings into my path when I've made such a mess of my life at times? How could I be, as the scripture says, "Qualified and made ... fit to share the portion which is the inheritance of the saints (God's holy people) in the Light?" I am not alone in believing the voice in my head that tries to convince me to get my act together before God can use me for anything. I have heard many people say that they have just too much stuff they must clean up before God can find them useful. Far too often we disqualify ourselves from allowing God to use us by believing we have nothing to offer. We believe that our past mistakes have made that impossible. I have heard it said by some, "Once I get things right in my life then I will think about getting right with God." That's not how it works. First God wants us to get right with Him and then He helps us get things right in our lives. That's when He qualifies us; when we allow Him to do the work! If you are a child of God you have been made sufficient and equipped with adequate power to perform the duties God has given you because He has assigned you a part. We have all been given a part to play for Him during our time here. It does not need to matter how big or how small the part, what matters is that we allow ourselves to play it. We must stop feeling inadequate and looking at our lack and embrace the fact that He desires to work through us. For many years I stood behind what someone else said about the Bible rather than what I read or believed simply because I did not feel qualified to voice my opinion. I remember many times when I would say, "So and so says this about the Lord," or, "So and so says this about the Word." One day while talking to a friend of mine she said, "I don't care what 'so and so' says. I want to know what *you* say." It was very hard for me to think that what I had to say had any influence. After all, what qualifications did I have when it came to knowing the Bible? We think that we need to attend Bible school or have some type of formal education before we share a verse of scripture. We disqualify ourselves by looking at our insufficiencies rather than considering what God can do with us. God is not searching for the person with the most degrees and trophies hanging on the wall, He desires the most willing. He is looking for those who love Him and believe that He is all His word tells us He is. Far too many people allow their minds to believe that all of their knowledge comes from the classes they have taken in college. Sure, college is a good and necessary tool in our lives that can bring about a great job, but God says that He has chosen the "foolish" rather than the wise!

> Remember, dear brothers and sisters, that few of you were wise in the world's eyes or powerful or wealthy when God called you. Instead, God chose things the world considers foolish in order to shame those who think they are wise. And He chose things that are powerless to shame those who are powerful. God chose things despised by the world; things counted as nothing at all, and used them to bring to nothing what the world considers important. As a result, no one can ever boast in the presence of God.
>
> 1 Corinthians 1:26

All of our boasting needs to be done in the Lord. Please recognize that without Jesus we aren't qualified for anything, much less a life of eternity with the King of Kings and Lord of Lords!

We have been qualified to inherit the same life that the Saints before us received and in Isaiah 61 we are given a few instructions as to what we are qualified to do.

The Spirit of the Lord God is upon me, because the Lord has anointed and *qualified* me to preach the Gospel of good tidings to the meek, the poor, and afflicted; He has sent me to bind up and heal the brokenhearted, to proclaim liberty to the [physical and spiritual] captives and the opening of the prison and of the eyes to those who are bound, To proclaim the acceptable year of the Lord [the year of His favor] and the day of vengeance of our God, to comfort all who mourn, To grant [consolation and joy] to those who mourn in Zion—to give them an ornament (a garland or diadem) of beauty instead of ashes, the oil of joy instead of mourning, the garment [expressive] of praise instead of a heavy, burdened, and failing spirit—that they may be called oaks of righteousness [lofty, strong, and magnificent, distinguished for uprightness, justice, and right standing with God], the planting of the Lord, that He may be glorified.

Isaiah 61:1-3 (Amplified Bible)

Tell your story! Tell the story of His grace in your life. Allow God to use you to help change the lives of those around you. No matter what you've been through, He wants to bring beauty from ashes, and He wants to use your life and all you have walked through to speak into the lives of those around you. Share His love. Reach out with His kindness and grace. Offer the same mercy that was offered to you to each person He brings your way. It is time to stop believing the lie that tells you, "You could not be used by God because _____." You are qualified; you share in the inheritance of all the saints! They had a story to tell, too. Can you imagine the day we meet in glory and can sit around the big banquet table and swap stories with the saints before us? Oh, what fun that will be! Practice up!

Questions to consider

1) Have you ever considered yourself to be a qualified Christian? How did you become qualified?

2) Do you believe God can and wants to use you in the lives of those around you to be an influence on them *for* Him?

3) Read Hebrews 11 and list the names and what the Bible tells us they did by faith. (You may want to use a blank piece of paper.) What can we learn from the saints?

4) Do you feel qualified to complete the task God might call you to?

5) Do you believe that God can speak to you through others? If yes, how well do you receive revelation from others? If not, how do you believe God speaks to you?

6) Is there something from your past that keeps you from believing that you can be/are qualified by God?

7) Read Romans 10:14-17. What does it have to say?

8) What risks have you taken in faith?

9) Read Philippians 2. What can we learn from verse four? What can we learn about Jesus from verses 8-11?

10) Of the disciples whom Jesus called, there was Peter (the outspoken one), Thomas (the doubter), John (laid his head on Jesus's chest), and Judas (the betrayer), among others. Which of the twelve would you say you identify with and why?

# R Is for Righteous

## God Says I am Righteous

For our sake He made Christ [virtually] to be sin Who knew no sin, so that in and through Him we might become [endued with, viewed as being in, and examples of] the *righteousness* of God [what we ought to be, approved and acceptable and in right relationship with Him, by His goodness].

2 Corinthians 5:21 (Amplified Bible)

*Righteous:* characterized by uprightness or morality; acting in an upright, moral way; virtuous. Righteousness: the quality or state of being righteous (dictionary.com, 2011).

Have you ever woken in the morning with one thought repeating itself over and over? One Saturday morning I awoke to the same statement running over and over in my mind. It was this; *It is time to put down the milk and start eating the meat.* Like a broken record it repeated over and over again. Later, while out walking with my husband, we were discussing several upsetting situations that were going on between Christians we knew. I shared with him the statement that had been repeating itself in my mind. We both began to have a sense that it was a message from the Lord, not only for us but the church as a whole. As we mulled over this statement and how it pertained to the situations we were walking through, we came to the conclusion that what the Lord was telling us was very simply this; it is time for His children to grow up! In other words, God wanted us to *mature* in the knowledge and understanding of the Word. As I look back on that time, I know without any doubt that is exactly what God was calling us to do. I also have no doubt that His desire and plan for every person who calls on Him in faith is the same. He wants us to mature in our faith and knowledge of who He is and what His Word really says.

When all three of our children were born, like most parents, we were thrilled. Each one was a new little life, so fragile and sweet, given to us by God to help raise and mold. They were precious to us and everything they did was just adorable. (Well, to us it was, anyway!) But we all know that children do not stay little forever.) Eventually they begin to grow, and what was adorable to us when they were babies might not be quite as cute anymore. They begin to learn and experience more of life, and changes are to be expected. They learn to let go of some items that they have found security in— like blankets and bottles. (I fondly recall our oldest son clinging to his "Globaby" for the first two years of his life.) As parents we want our kids to learn how to go from a bottle to a cup. How ridiculous would it be if a twenty-year-old man still drank from a baby bottle? Or if our son, now as a grown man, still carried his Globaby around with him? In the same way, while it is good for them to drink only milk as infants, eventually their bodies need more nourishment from solid food, so parents slowly introduce them to rice and fruits and vegetables. A parent's desire for their children is that, as a child grows, they put away childish behaviors and mature. If we want this for our children, what makes us believe that our Heavenly Father would not want the same for His children?

Paul wrote this in his letter to the Corinthian church, "Brothers and sisters, I could not address you as people who live by the Spirit but as people who are still worldly—mere infants in Christ. I gave you milk, not solid food, for you were not yet ready for it. Indeed, you are still not ready" (1 Corinthians 3:1-2). In the book of Hebrews we find this admonition:

> For even though by this time you ought to be teaching others, you actually need someone to teach you over again the very first principles of God's Word. You have come to need milk, not solid food. For everyone who continues to feed on milk is obviously inexperienced and unskilled in the doctrine of righteousness (of conformity to the divine will in purpose, thought, and action), for he is a mere infant [not able to talk yet]! But solid food is for full-grown men, for those whose senses and mental faculties are trained by practice to discriminate and distinguish between what is morally good and noble and what is evil and contrary either to divine or human law.
>
> Hebrews 5:12-14 (Amplified Bible)

In *Erdmann's Handbook of the Bible,* I read that the book of Hebrews was written to a...

> ...group of Jewish Christians. They were men of some intellectual ability. The group had been established a good many years, and had a history of persecution. They should have been mature Christians by this time, capable of teaching others. Instead, they are withdrawn and inward-looking. And they seem to have half a mind to turn back to Judaism. They need a forceful reminder that what they possess in Christ is far better.
>
> Alexander (1992)

Because this group had not grown from infancy in the Word to maturity in the Word, they received a letter of correction.

We must pray and ask God to show us if we are growing and maturing in His Word and in knowledge of that Word according to His plan for our lives.

At this point you may be wondering what maturity has to do with righteousness. In Psalm 4 we are told to, "Offer the sacrifices of righteousness, and put your trust in the Lord" (Psalm 4:5). A small child has a very hard time with sacrifice. They don't want to let go of whatever object they may be holding on to. The tears flow heavily when an attempt is made to remove anything from their possession. As we grow and mature in Christ we soon discover that offering the sacrifices of righteousness means just that- sacrifice. We must lay down anything that causes us to live an unrighteous life. When God begins to challenge us to grow, do we refuse and remain an infant in the Word, or do we press in to the challenge and move forward to maturity? You may ask; "How is that possible?"

As I began to really press into the verse in 2 Corinthians from the Amplified Bible, I saw righteousness begin to form in my heart and mind.

> For our sake He made Christ [virtually] to be sin Who knew no sin, so that in and through Him we might become [endued with, viewed as being in, and examples of] the righteousness of God [what we ought to be, approved and acceptable and in right relationship with Him, by His goodness].
>
> 2 Corinthians 5:21

Let's look once again at this remarkable gift Jesus gave to us. For our benefit He became sin. He did not just take our sin on Him; He *became* sin. Can you imagine? The entire world's sin—past, present, and future; He embodied all that sin. I know how heavy the weight of sin can be on me when I go against what I know is right. I can't begin to imagine how tormented He must have been with the weight of that consuming Him. The reason? So we could become the righteousness of God. Amazing!

I love that the Amplified Bible says that we might become *endued with, viewed as being in and examples of...* the righteousness of God. We are the righteousness of God, and because that's what we *are,* that's what we portray to all those around us. The word endued means "to invest or endow with some gift, quality, or faculty or to put on; assume" (dictionary.com, 2011). Is it safe to say the righteousness of God has been *put on* us? We inherit God's righteousness when we accept Jesus as our Savior and Lord. He puts His righteousness upon us. In the same way my husband may put his coat upon me on a chilly night, Jesus put His own righteousness upon me.

So how, then, do we begin walking in righteousness and what does it look like? What steps can we take to make sure we are growing and maturing so we can be examples of Christ's righteousness? Here are a few examples the Lord has shown me through my time with Him. Romans 6:13 says, "Do not offer the parts of your body to sin, as instruments of wickedness, but rather offer yourselves to God, as those who have been brought from death to life; and offer the parts of your body to him as instruments of righteousness."

First, offer yourself to God. As we discussed previously, begin to make Him number one in your life. As you seek to grow in your relationship with Him, it is important to belong to a church that teaches the Word of God in its full truth. Find a *solid* Bible teacher to sit under for instruction. Proverbs 14:7 tells us to, "Go from the presence of a foolish man, when you do not perceive in him the lips of knowledge." Paul told Timothy to:

> Preach the word; be prepared in season and out of season; correct, rebuke and encourage—with great patience and

careful instruction. For the time will come when people will not put up with sound doctrine. Instead, to suit their own desires, they will gather around them a great number of teachers to say what their itching ears want to hear. They will turn their ears away from the truth and turn aside to myths.

2 Timothy 4:2-4

A good, solid Bible teacher will not be afraid of speaking hard things to the congregation and we must seek after sound doctrine. Yes, our toes might get stepped on from time to time, and we might feel uncomfortable, but allowing the sting of truth from the conviction of the Holy Spirit helps us grow and mature. If the Pastor has taught sound doctrine on a social issue that opposes the worldview, how will we respond? Will we write him a letter following the service expressing our disapproval of his message? We might decide we no longer agree with the churches doctrine and leave. Or we resolve that it is time for the Pastor to be moved to a new church. We must not shy away from knowing the truth of His Word and how it pertains to our lives. Allow the Spirit's conviction to bring about the maturing in our lives God intended so we can walk in righteousness. Paul wrote to the Colossians,

For this reason, since the day we heard about you, we have not stopped praying for you and asking God to fill you with the knowledge of His will through all spiritual wisdom and understanding. And we pray this in order that you may live a life worthy of the Lord and may please Him in every way: bearing fruit in every good work, growing in the knowledge of God.

Colossians 1:9-10

We reveal God's righteousness to the world around us through our behavior and our speech, thoughts, and actions. We have the ability, because Christ made it possible, to be examples of Christ's righteousness because we *are* His righteousness. So when we are told to live a life worthy of the Lord, pleasing Him, growing in Him and bearing fruit for Him, we can, if we are willing to offer the sacrifice of righteousness to Him.

How can we be examples of righteous behavior to those around us? What comes out of our mouths can be a great place to start. Psalm 37:30 instructs us that, "The mouth of the [uncompromisingly] righteous utters wisdom, and his tongue speaks with justice" (Amplified Bible). We are directed in Ephesians 4 to,

> Let no foul or polluting language, nor evil word nor unwholesome or worthless talk [ever] come out of your mouth, but only such [speech] as is good and beneficial to the spiritual progress of others, as is fitting to the need and the occasion, that it may be a blessing and give grace (God's favor) to those who hear it.
>
> Ephesians 4:29

I love that the Amplified Bible places the word, uncompromisingly, before the word righteous. We must always be alert as God's righteous ones, considering our actions; compromise is costly to a Christian. Psalm 34:15 from the Amplified Bible tells us, "The eyes of the Lord are toward the [uncompromisingly] righteous and His ears are open to their cry." The Father has good plans and desires for His children and we do ourselves an injustice when we do not take the necessary steps to understand His ways. We live in spiritual poverty when we compromise His Word. Psalm 5:12 says, "For You, Lord, will bless the [uncompromisingly] righteous [him who is upright and in right standing with You]; as with a shield You will surround him with goodwill (pleasure and favor)" (Amplified Bible). There are so many promises tucked in the Word it would be impossible to list them all here. Are we living far below the level in which He desires for us to live through compromise? What areas of righteous behavior are we quick to allow compromise in? How we dress? How we spend our time? The movies we watch and the books we read? Simply because "everyone" is doing it, watching it, wearing it, or reading it does not make it acceptable to God's righteous children. Remember, offer the sacrifice of righteousness and say, "no thank you."

Oh, friends, let's become secure enough in our true identity, which is one who has become *the righteousness of God,* so that we can cast aside all sin. Let's always ask God to help us behave in the same righteous manner He would. Psalm 23:3b says, "He guides me in paths of righteousness for His name's sake." It is for His fame and His glory, His name's sake, that we should allow Him to guide us in that path. Not for ours. Let's make today the day of change. Let this be the day when we determine to set aside all compromise and allow His righteousness to flow through us and out to a world in need of His truth.

Questions to consider:

1) How have you matured in your relationship with the Lord?

2) Has the process of "growing up" in the Lord been a long one for you?

3) How would you characterize the differences in a baby Christian from a mature believer?

4) In Psalm 37:25, David makes a statement about his view of God's faithfulness to the righteous. What did he say?

5)   When faced with the trials and tribulations of every day life, how can we respond out of our righteousness rather than react out of our own fleshly nature?

6)   What is God's promise in Psalm 106:3 to those who do what is right? (If you have opportunity, read this verse in the Amplified Bible)

7)   Many verses of the Amplified have the word *uncompromisingly* before the word *righteous*. Why do you suppose that is? What does the word compromise mean?

8)   We must be careful to not compromise God's Word in any way. How do we compromise God's Word? How do you compromise His Word?

9)   What does Proverbs 21:3 say, and what do you think the Lord wants you to understand by it?

10)  The definition of righteousness in the Greek lists these words: integrity, virtue, purity of life, rightness, correctness of thinking, feeling, and acting. How does each word play out in the life of believer? Why are they important? What difference can they make in the lives of non-believers?

# S Is for Secure

## God Says I am Secure

"Lord, you alone are my portion and my cup; you make my lot *secure*."

Psalm 6:5

*Secure*: free from or not exposed to danger or harm; safe, in safe custody or keeping, free from care; without anxiety (dictionary. com, 2011).

While visiting family for the Christmas holiday one year I did my own little survey. I asked several of my family members these three questions:

1) How would you define the word secure?

2) What makes you feel secure?

3) Where do people find security these days?

Every person answered the first question with the word *safe* in his or her answer. When people have a sense of safety, they feel secure. When threatened in any way, security is lost. This only makes sense, after all, since one of the definitions of secure is *safe.* Relationships and finances were popular answers to question number two. We often find security in our relationships, our marriages, and our money. Our friends or spouses make us feel secure, and the more money we have in the bank the more secure we feel we are. As for the answers to the third question, they, of course, varied. There was a common thread to the answers, which led me to understand that people find security in many different ways. The answers included sex, drugs, alcohol, money, food, religion, material things, status, and popularity. It is very true that we have many different options these days in what we can seek after in our quest for security. We may think, *If I only made more money or have this much money saved, then I would feel secure.* I know some people who must have their bank account at a certain amount, or else they do not believe they are secure. Sometimes I struggle with the weight thought, *If I could only lose a few pounds, I would feel more secure with myself.*

People try to find security in their talents and abilities, but that leads me to wonder, what happens when the time comes and the talents can no longer be used? If a professional athlete obtains all his or her security in what they can do in the game, what happens to them when they no longer can play the game? We have watched as athletes have retired, returned to the sport, or even a new one, and then retire again, struggling to let go of the position they held in the sports world.

As women it is very easy to seek our security in our work, a man, or friendships. Some even seek security in no one other than themselves, believing that they can never trust anyone. We often hear women make the comment, "I just have to do it myself because I cannot trust anyone else will do it as well." I have also known women that go to the other extreme, desiring to have a man in their life lest they felt completely lost. When one relationship does not work out, they quickly move on to the next. If we try to gain our security from our friendships, we can become very possessive to the extent of allowing ourselves to become jealous when we have to share our friends with others. I remember my high school days and the drama that came from jealousy in friendships. I relived it all with my daughter and her high school days, too. I also had a friend who once struggled with this issue in our friendship. Placing our security in our friendships will lead to heartache when life takes a turn or the Lord requires a move.

There have been many times that I have tried to find security in my friendships, in money, in my marriage, in a job, in health, and in possessions only to discover I still have a need for something more. I have come to realize that when life begins to get a little bit rocky and I reach out to steady myself to find the security I desire, I had better reach for Jesus, because what I reach for may just be what ruins me. It has happened not only to me but also to people I know and love. When life began to get the best of them they reached out to alcohol or drugs, and some even found their comfort in food. We may reach out to the arms of someone other than our spouse, while others simply walk away from the commitment of their family altogether. There are those who become obsessed with money—some with work and their position and the power they feel they have there. Many of us find security in having lots of possessions, running up large debt that we could not possibly pay,spending money we don't have so we can own the best of everything. We make sure we and our kids, wear the finest of the name brand clothing and we do whatever activity we desire until one day when we discover ourselves drowning in such debt that bankruptcy is the only option out. I have known people who are so caught up in wanting to be popular that they were willing to forsake their own moral standards to fit in. Our society is riddled with alcoholics, drug abusers, and an ever-increasing obese population. According to the US Census Bureau issued in 2009, 26.3 percent of all children under twenty-one years of age live with one parent (Grall, 2009). We have more things, opportunities, and money than our ancestors ever had, yet statistics show that one in four women will experience severe depression at some point in their lives (Schoenstadt, 2009). I look around and I wonder; could it be possible that we are looking for security in all the wrong places? Or maybe we just do not understand what real security means. If having more things or making more money can truly bring about the security I am seeking and longing for, why do I still struggle with insecurity when I add more stuff to my collection? I've tried seeking security in things and people, and I've come to realize that the place I have found the most security is when I am standing firmly on the foundation of God's Word.

I was the type of person who was always living for the moment, seeking and searching for the next thing that would satisfy, when I came upon this verse in Ecclesiastes 3:11.

> He has made everything beautiful in its time. He also has planted eternity in men's hearts and minds [a divinely implanted sense of a purpose working through the ages which nothing under the sun but God alone can satisfy], yet so that men cannot find out what God has done from the beginning to the end.
>
> Ecclesiastes 3:11 (Amplified Bible)

He has planted eternity in our hearts and minds, and nothing but God alone can ever truly satisfy. We can search and try to find satisfaction through anything other than God, but with eternity planted within us there will always be a sense of something missing if we do not surrender ourselves to Him. Oftentimes it takes a shaking of our foundation for us to realize that sense of eternity that has been planted in our hearts. The death of a loved one brings us to a standstill as we contemplate eternal realities. The terrorist attacks on 9/11 brought us, once again, to a place of questioning our security. One man's dishonest greed took a combined $17,000,000,000 from victims who thought they were investing for the future (Katersky, 2011). There is so much instability in the world right now that if we perceive these circumstances only through our natural eyes we certainly will become filled with fear and lose all hope. We need God to help us walk through life's tragedies, holding on to the promises He has made in His Word. One of the promises I hold close to my heart is found in Psalm 37:18-19. "Day by day the Lord takes care of the innocent, and they will receive an inheritance that lasts forever. They will not be disgraced in hard times; even in famine they will have more than enough." Not everything in life is always going to go right. If we lose ourselves to despair when life gets hard, and looks as though everything is falling apart, then our security has been tragically misplaced. Proverbs 24:10 tells us, "If you falter in a time of trouble, how small is your strength!" Our adversary wants us to take our eyes off of God in times of trouble and put them on the situations around us, forgetting that God is in control of everything and that He is much bigger than your worst day.

When God brought the Israelites to the Promised Land, He instructed Moses to send men to explore it and bring back a detailed report of the land. What they found was indeed a land flowing with milk and honey, grapes, pomegranates, and figs. But what they also saw were the descendants of Anak, Amalekites, the Hittites, the Jebusites, and the Amorites, and that's all it took to give a bad report to the Children of Israel.

> Then Caleb quieted the people before Moses, and said, "Let us go up at once and take possession, for we are well able to overcome it." But the men who had gone up with him said, "We are not able to go up against the people, for they are stronger than we." And they gave the children of Israel a bad report of the land which they had spied out, saying, "The land through which we have gone as spies is a land that devours its inhabitants, and all the people whom

we saw in it are men of great stature. There we saw the
giants (the descendants of Anak came from the giants);
and we were like grasshoppers in our own sight, and so we
were in their sight."

Numbers 13:30-33

Who they saw themselves as and who they were in God's eyes were
two very different descriptions. God told them they could take the
land because He had given it to them, but they refused to even try
because with their own natural eyes they were small grasshoppers
and unable to do it. We must be careful when God desires to bless
us that we do not miss out because the task looks bigger than what
we believe we are able to overcome. When Joshua and Caleb tried
to convince the Israelites that they could go into the land because
God had given it to them, they wanted to stone them. We can take
on that attitude at times, can we not? When we are full of fear in a
situation and someone walks in with a word of encouragement or
hope, we would rather stone the person than find comfort in his
or her words. Having a strong foundation built upon the Word of
God will help us when the storms of life come at us. We just need
to make sure that our foundation is not full of cracks.

One summer day I was walking around the outside of our
home when I noticed that our foundation wall seemed to have a
slight angle to it. I thought it looked very strange and mentioned
it to my husband. He couldn't see it. I mentioned it to my parents
when they were visiting. My mother saw it, but my father did not.
So we ignored it until it could no longer be ignored. While painting
the walls in our finished basement, I noticed that the outside wall
did not feel right, nor did it look right. I began to see, as I started
my investigation, a bow to the wall and that the chair rail molding
was pushed apart. I began to notice that the sheetrock had cracked
and moved. Finally our worst fears were realized when we took the
cover off of the area that holds our water pipes. Our foundation
wall was cracked all the way down the middle. The wall was actually

lying against our water pipes with a crack about an inch wide. From one end of the house to the other the foundation wall had split and moved. The weight of it had also shifted the end wall. There was another huge crack that went from top to bottom at the end of the house. Once we discovered the cracked foundation wall, we noticed walls within the house that were showing signs of the stress the crack had created. A crack here and there, a slight bowing in the middle, even the rug in one of the rooms had been moved back. We hadn't noticed these before, but now we realized that our entire house was at risk because of the broken foundation wall. We called contractor after contractor to look at the wall and could not find many willing to take on the job. "Too big" and "too risky" were comments we heard over and over again. We began to pray and ask the Lord to show us how He was going to work this all out. While we were in the midst of praying I began to learn the importance of a strong foundation. Just as the homes in which we live must be built on a strong foundation if they are going to stand, our faith must also be built on a strong foundation, or in times of crisis it, too, will not stand.

In Luke 6:47-49 we are told the importance of a strong foundation.

> As for everyone who comes to me and hears my words and puts them into practice, I will show you what they are like. They are like a man building a house, who dug down deep and laid the foundation on rock. When a flood came, the torrent struck that house but could not shake it, because it was well built. But the one who hears my words and does not put them into practice is like a man who built a house on the ground without a foundation. The moment the torrent struck that house, it collapsed and its destruction was complete.
>
> Luke 6:47-49

Our house is built on clay soil, which holds water and is very, very hard. We also live in the snow belt and get a *ton* of snow in the winters. To save ourselves from shoveling snow off the roof, years ago we put a metal roof on the house, not realizing that our foundation was weak. Winter after winter the snow and ice—in feet—would slide off our roof and land in front of the house. Let me tell you, it sounds and feels like elephants are running down our roof when it lets loose. Due to the fact that the foundation wall was built wrong right from the start, it was not strong enough to endure the beating it took year after year. Thankfully, the Lord led us to wise counsel and we were able to repair the wall for much less than we had been quoted. We learned the value of a strong foundation through the entire process—a foundation that is properly built can withstand the pressures that come at it from the outside. One that is poorly laid and improperly built can give you a false sense of security and when the troubles of this life hit, and they can hit hard, nothing is there to hold you up.

God has proven that He is faithful to me time and time again. I know that true security is found here on earth when we have our foundation planted firmly on the promises of the Word. No matter what the circumstance, God is more than enough. He has everything under control and nothing is a surprise to Him. I have had to say many times, "Well God, this wasn't part of my plan, but I know You have a plan. Please show me what it is!" Psalm 33:20 says, "Our soul waits for the Lord; He is our help and our shield." I know that God has a good grip on me and He's not letting me go, no matter what.

> My sheep hear My voice, and I know them, and they follow Me. And I give them eternal life, and they shall never perish; neither shall anyone snatch them out of My hand. My Father, who has given them to Me, is greater than all; and no one is able to snatch them out of My Father's hand.
>
> John 10:27-29

What a wonderful promise we have been given. My life is in His hands, and I know that one day my time here on earth will end, and I will begin the rest of my days, all of eternity, with Him in Glory. I have a sign in my office. It is an acronym that spells out the word *alive,* and it says this, "Always Living In View of Eternity." It reminds me to keep my feet planted on the foundation of God's Word and my eyes lifted to the One who knows how to handle every circumstance I face. Plant your feet and lift your eyes.

Questions to consider:

1) How would you define security? What makes you feel secure?

2) What do you view yourself as: a grasshopper or a giant?

3) Read Proverbs 1. Who calls out to us in verse 20? Who are we told to listen to in verse 33? What will we find if we do?

4) Where can we find wisdom?

5) Read Proverbs 10:9. What brings security?

6) Where would you say your foundation is built? On Christ or in the natural?

7) Often we find security in money and prosperity. Read Joshua 1:7-9. What are the instructions given? What makes your way prosperous? What brings success?

8) Read 2 Kings 18:1-8. What did Hezekiah do that allowed him to prosper according to verse 6?

9)  How do you hold fast to the Lord and not depart from Him?

10) Read 2 Samuel 22. What are some of the names David uses to describe God? Is He all those to you? If not, how can He become your Shield? Your Stronghold?

# T IS FOR TREASURED

## God Says I am Treasured

"The Lord has declared today that you are his people, his own special *treasure*, just as He promised, and that you must obey all His commands."

Deuteronomy 26:18 (NLT)

*Treasure*: any thing or person greatly valued or highly prized (dictionary.com, LLC, 2011).

I love to collect old things. I just love to shop at little antique stores, hunting for a treasure. While I am hunting and picking up items I find so interesting, my husband is usually standing around, rolling his eyes, praying I don't say, "I want this!" I always remind him, "One man's junk is another man's treasure!" As I have allowed the scripture from Deuteronomy to roll around in my heart, it has made me think about that statement, "One man's junk is another man's treasure," and how it relates to friendship. It may seem odd to compare the two, but in recent months I have been witness to the pain that people experience in broken relationships. It has caused me to spend time with the Lord, praying for healing for those who have been hurt so badly and also has made me wonder, *If we call ourselves friends then how can friends treat each other this way?* I know I, too, have experienced the pain of feeling more like trash that is easily thrown away than anyone's treasure. Too many times I have seen the tears and heard the broken hearts as we try to understand how those closest to us could just walk away from a friendship. At times I struggle when I sense a friendship is going through change. Letting go is very hard for me yet I realize there are times when a friend may move out of your life simply because of the changes brought about by time and circumstance. There are times when there is no need for any type of explanation as to why the friendship has changed. But there have been times when I have experienced the rejection of a friend and had no understanding or explanation as to why. In fact, I still wonder. There have also been moments when I have been treated to a very long and descriptive list of my faults and failures as a friend, which gave complete understanding as to why the friendship was going to change. Since the people in our lives do not always make us feel very "treasured," I believe we can have a very hard time accepting that we are valued and treasured by God. There is such comfort for me, and I pray for you as well, knowing that we are never considered junk to God but instead He treasures us. He places great value on us; in fact, I happen to know that we are the apple of His eye (Psalm 17:8)! He treasures everything about us. He treasures the time we spend with Him, our love for Him, and our friendship with Him. Unlike us humans who have a tendency to remove people from our lives rather easily, He never walks away from us. He does not get mad at us, does not hold grudges, and does not hold failures over us. He is not easily offended, and He is always there for us. His promise is that He will never leave us nor forsake us (Deuteronomy 31:8, Hebrews 13:5). One scripture I find encouraging is in John 15, where Jesus calls you and me, *friend.* "I no longer call you servants, because a servant does not know his master's business. Instead, I have called you friends, for everything that I learned from My Father I have made known to you."

That statement, in my opinion, is a great measure of friendship. He is willing to share everything He knows with us, His friends. Through the Word I believe we can learn a lot about friendship. We can discover what His desire is for us in having friends and why we need them. We can use the Word to help us understand what a healthy friendship should look like. We can gain insight into whom He desires for us to spend our time with and how we can treasure those we call friends. It is true that everything He learned from His Father He has made known to us.

Some of the deepest wounds I have carried came at the hands of people whom I considered to be my closest friends. I can also be honest and tell you that I know that I have also caused pain to some of my friends, as well. I'm sure that most of the time the wounds we cause others is unintentional. But there are times when our intent is to cause suffering. We become upset, hurt, and angry and do not try to hide it. Recently I have watched two people, who are very close to me, walk through the pain of "friendship," and I've realized that sometimes we just do not know how to be good friends. Misunderstanding and lack of communication can create terrible tension in a friendship. Jealousy and insecurity will devastate it, and anger and un-forgiveness will destroy it. Hebrews 12:15 warns us, "See to it that no one misses the grace of God and that no bitter root grows up to cause trouble and defile many." We must remember that Satan loves to steal, kill, and destroy; that's his job (John 10:10). He likes to create tension in our relationships. If he can devastate someone through a broken relationship, he will try. Whatever he can do to destroy our relationships with one another, he is going to attempt it. We must remember that he is like a roaring lion, seeking to devour (1 Peter 5:8). So we must be watchful and not allow Satan to get a foothold in our relationships with one another. We must seek to know and understand how God works in our relationships and what He is doing behind the scenes in each one of us.

There is no doubt that God wants us to have good friends, and He wants us to be a good friend. Ecclesiastes 4:9 confirms this by stating, "Two are better than one, because they have a good reward for their labor. For if they fall, one will lift up his companion. But woe to him who is alone when he falls, for he has no one to help him up."

God wants us to realize that He never intended for us to go through life alone. He reveals that to us in Genesis when He said, "It is not good that man should be alone; I will make him a helper comparable to him" (Genesis 2:18). He gave Eve to Adam because He knew that it was not good to be alone. Sometimes we allow selfishness, bitterness, and our own stubbornness to become our best friends, and we push people right out of our lives. The Lord says woe to them who do this because they are alone, and if you are alone, you have no one to help when you fall. We all fall and we all need help, no matter what we choose to believe. How can we strive to be a good friend and learn to treasure those whom God has placed in our lives? The Word tells us if we want to have friends, we must first be a good friend. "A man who has friends must himself be friendly" (Proverbs 18:24a). We are warned, "The righteous should choose his friends carefully, for the way of the wicked leads them astray" (Proverbs 12:26). We also read in First Corinthians 15:33 that "bad company corrupts good character." Who we choose to have around us is very important to God, and it should be important to us. Spending time with others who are like-minded matters. Paul tells us in Philippians 2:1-3,

> If you have any encouragement from being united with Christ, if any comfort from his love, if any fellowship with the Spirit, if any tenderness and compassion, then make my joy complete by being like-minded, having the same love, being one in spirit and purpose.

Way back in the early days of my walk, as you know, I had an anger problem. I had a *big* anger problem. I remember reading a scripture one day when I was really struggling with anger towards one of my friends. It is found in Proverbs and the Lord used it to really convict my heart. It says, "Make no friendship with an angry man, and with a furious man do not go, lest you learn his ways and set a snare for your soul" (Proverbs 22:24&25). As someone who really struggled with anger issues, I saw myself so clearly in this verse, and I realized that if my friends read that verse and obeyed it, like they should, they could very easily tell me, "I cannot go with you as a friend any longer. I may learn your ways and get caught in the snare of anger." (As I think on that now, maybe that's why I lost some of my friends!) It was always much easier for me to hold onto un-forgiveness than to let people off the hook. I *was* a person who was easily offended. Do you know anyone like that?

We live in a society where people become easily offended. Just listen to the news every night and you can easily see who has been offended by something said or done by one person (or group) to another. People turn innocent statements upside down and inside out, looking for a reason to be offended. Have we forgotten how to believe the best in one another? It is not very often that you hear someone say, "I'm sure they did not mean anything by it." In our relationships we need to begin to believe the best of one another. We must overcome the tendency we have to be hurt and offended easily. Friendships are destroyed when we don't allow ourselves to forgive quickly, overcome the offense, and move on from it. "He who covers and forgives an offense seeks love, but he who repeats or harps on a matter separates even close friends" (Proverbs 17:9). I know from experience it is impossible to be in relationships that require you to watch every word you say and everything you do. I am not perfect, and sometimes—okay, often—I am going to slip up. I need my friends to understand that I mean no harm to them; I need them to believe the best of me. I need the people in my life to be willing to cover my sins with grace, love, and mercy.

A good friend learns how to let go of things quickly, without taking offense often, and they don't keep score. I have learned that the battle begins right away when a careless word is spoken or a thoughtless act is done. It is then that we must choose to let it go or talk about it with the one who hurt us. Sometimes we can get over it without a word spoken, but there are times when hurts need to be taken care of. If you have been hurt by someone and are unable to move beyond it, then chances are you need to talk to them about it. Keeping conflicts buried inside oftentimes will lead to an explosion of gigantic proportions that could have been prevented had the matter been discussed when it first happened. "The beginning of strife is as when water first trickles [from a crack in a dam]; therefore stop contention before it becomes worse and quarreling breaks out" (Proverbs 17:14, Amplified Bible). We must be careful that we do not allow strife to fester inside for too long. There is much damage done if we do.

We can learn an important lesson about friendship from Exodus 33. In verse 11 we can see the intimate relationship God had with Moses. "So the Lord spoke to Moses face to face, as a man speaks to his friend." Good friends speak to one another face to face, not behind backs *about* one another. When we refuse to deal with our offenses toward one another it becomes very easy to talk about the person you are upset with. Our social networking sights have become a way for us to expose our grievances about someone without ever facing them. It is not always easy to go to a friend and talk to them about a hurt that you could not get over, but it is an act of love that God established for us to do. I am indebted to the good friends who have been faithful to speak truth to me no matter how painful it was to hear at the moment. Proverbs 27:6 is a scripture that I have found comfort in and appreciated—when used correctly! It lets us know this powerful truth, "Wounds from a sincere friend are better than many kisses from an enemy." None of us are perfect, and we all have areas that need to be worked on. Our sincere and loyal friends aren't going to just allow us to do whatever and say whatever; they are going to hold us accountable. We know those who are in our lives that we can trust to tell us the truth, and sometimes the truth hurts! People who are always telling us what we want to hear, well, they really aren't good friends, and they really aren't doing us any favors. A good friend tells us what we *need* to hear, not just what we *want* to hear. When we have friends that we are willing to be honest with and accountable to, the Word promises that, "As iron sharpens iron, so a man sharpens the countenance of his friend" (Proverbs 27:17.)

The Bible tells us that a wonderful characteristic of a good friend is just that—loyalty. "A friend is always loyal, and a brother is born to help in time of need" (Proverbs 17:17). Another word for loyalty is faithfulness, and a good friend is faithful, especially in times of need. There have been times in my life when my closest friends have known my need before I did. I once felt so broken that I did not believe I could ever recover, yet God, in His mercy, sent a faithful friend to help in that time of need. There is nothing like having a treasured friend beside you, helping you when you are walking through the storms of life. We need to have loyal friends to walk beside us, and we must be loyal to those God has put in our lives, as well.

Jesus was a great model for us in relationships. He chose twelve disciples, and then of the twelve there were three that were chosen to go with Him up to the Mountain of Transfiguration. But even still, of the three, there was one that laid his head on Jesus's chest. In the same way, we may have a circle of twelve around us and of the twelve there may be three that we have a closer relationship with. Of the three we find the *one*. This is the one we can laugh with, cry with and share our secrets with, knowing we can always lay our head upon their chest for comfort.

One of the important lessons I have learned is that people do come and go out of our lives, and we must hold one another with an open hand. God will bring people into and out of our lives. He has a purpose for every individual He brings us in contact with. He wants us to learn from one another and be willing to teach one another. I am thankful for the people the Lord brought into my life to help me grow and mature in my relationship with Him and with others. I am extremely grateful for those who were able to see beyond my faults and into my heart, knowing that God was doing a work in me. Some have stuck with me, and others have walked away. I appreciate those who forgave me when I messed up, and I am thankful that the Lord has taught me how to forgive. I will always treasure what each has brought to my life just as God treasures what we can bring to the lives of others. I am so thankful for the friendship we have in Jesus. What a friend He is. As I finish this up I hear a sweet, old hymn whispering in my ear. Sing along with me, why don't ya?

What a friend we have in Jesus, all our sins and griefs to bear! What a privilege to carry everything to God in prayer! O what peace we often forfeit, O what needless pain we bear, all because we do not carry everything to God in prayer. Have we trials and temptations? Is there trouble anywhere? We should never be discouraged; take it to the Lord in prayer. Can we find a friend so faithful? Who will all our sorrows share? Jesus knows our every weakness; take it to the Lord in prayer. Are we weak and heavy laden, cumbered with a load of care? Precious Savior, still our refuge; take it to the Lord in prayer. Do thy friends despise, forsake thee? Take it to the Lord in prayer! In His arms He'll take and shield thee; thou wilt find a solace there.

Scriven

Questions to consider:

1) Do you believe it matters who your friends are?

2) How do friendships influence people?

3) How would you explain your relationship with Jesus? Would you say He is a Personal Friend, Acquaintance, or a Religious Figure?

4) Read 1 Samuel 18:1-4. What happened to David and Jonathon that made them such good friends? (Verse 1)

5) In verse 3, what did David and Jonathon do to secure their friendship?

6) In verse 4, Jonathon does something that shows he holds nothing back from his friend. What is it?

7) Read 1 Samuel 20. What happens in verse 16?

8) Where did Jonathon's loyalties lie?

9) What does the word covenant mean?

10) What does a covenant friendship mean?

11) Read John 15:13. What did Jesus do for us as a friend?

12) We may never be asked to lay down our lives, but what practical ways can we be good friends?

13) Do you have a friend that is willing to wound you for your own good?

# U Is for Understand

## God Says I am *Understood*

"Behold! God is mighty, and yet despises no one nor regards anything as trivial; He is mighty in power of *understanding* and heart."

Job 36:5

*Understand*: to be thoroughly familiar with; apprehend clearly the character, nature, or subtleties of (dictionary.com, LLC, 2011).

At the time I was writing this devotional study, two of my Bible study gals and I were sitting down each week working through each letter. When the letter U came upon us we were watching news coverage of earthquakes that were devastating other countries. Our hearts were breaking for the losses that people were enduring. One thought that came to our minds repeatedly was, "How can we possibly understand what life is like in the midst of such devastation?" After all, we each had woken up that morning from a peaceful night's sleep. I had slept soundly the night before in my cozy bed with my new flannel sheets. We can watch the news and see the suffering and sorrow, but is it possible to fully understand such tragedy when we have not endured it? I don't think it is. Not until I walk through a similar situation will I fully be able to grasp and understand the emotions that such great loss brings. But thankfully there is One who can. Only God alone can completely understand each man's heart in the wake of suffering. And only God alone can bring wholeness and healing once again to those who are brokenhearted. Psalm 147:3 tells us, "He heals the brokenhearted and binds up their wounds." The Hebrew word for *bind* is *chabash* and can be translated to "bandage." Can you imagine? God can bandage your wounds. If you allow Him to, that's just what He will do.

When we put a bandage on a wound we cover the wound to protect it from infection. While the wound is covered we can't see the healing process taking place beneath the bandage, but we trust that it is being done. We may sneak a peak every so often to observe the healing process and change the bandage, but it's best to leave a bandage on until the healing is complete. If we take the bandage off too early there is a chance that germs will get in the wound, and infection can set in, making matters worse. Once infection sets in, it takes much longer for the healing to be completed. That's how God's healing works; He is the bandage that covers our wounded hearts. We may not see the work being done underneath the surface, but we can trust that He is there, doing what only He alone can do, meeting us as only He can. If we don't allow Him to complete the healing work as He desires, infections can set it. Infections like bitterness, anger, resentment, cynicism, depression, and rebellion are all types of infections that the Lord does not want for us. He knows the pain of suffering, and as the Great Physician He wants to heal the wounds that can easily bring infections to our hearts. The only possible way this can happen, however, is if we allow Him access to our pain.

When we think that it is impossible for anyone to understand the pain of suffering, all we must do is pick up the Bible and read the book of Job. God will bring comfort to our hearts through the counsel of others who have suffered, and Job's story is one where comfort can be found.

Job was a man, a very prosperous man, who lived in the land of Uz. He "feared God and shunned evil." He had a great family, many possessions, and a very large household (Job 1:1-3). We would look at Job today and say, "That man has it all!" Until one day when Satan presented himself before the Lord, and the Lord asked him this question, "Have you considered my servant, Job, that there is none like him on the earth, a blameless and upright man, one who fears God and shuns evil?" (Job 1:8). Well, Satan had an answer to God about why Job was so good.

> Does Job fear God for nothing? Have You not made a hedge around him, around his household, and around all that he has on every side? You have blessed the work of his hands, and his possessions have increased in the land. But now, stretch out Your hand and touch all that he has, and he will surely curse You to Your face!
>
> Job 1:10-11

Satan set a challenge before God that if Job lost everything he had he would no longer be the man God thought he was. So the Lord told Satan that all Job had was in his power and he could do whatever he wished but he could not lay a hand on Job himself. In one day Job lost his livestock and servants, his house, and his children. My heart aches with pain when I try to imagine Job's sorrow that day. I imagine those who have endured losing all they value most at the hands of natural disasters can relate very well to Job's suffering. Verse 20 says that he "arose, tore his robe and shaved his head; and he fell to the ground and worshipped." And then he said, "The Lord has given and the Lord has taken away. Blessed be the name of the Lord" (verse 21). Verse 22 tells us that "in all this, Job did not sin nor charge God with wrong." That verse always jumps right out at me when I read it. In all Job's suffering, he never sinned against God or charged God with wrong. I have yet to witness a tragedy where someone affected by it has not charged God with wrong and blamed Him for the wrong that has been done to them. I know that I charged God with wrong when my brother-in-law died. I know many people who have a bone to pick with God over the suffering they have endured. We may not even have a close relationship with God, but when something bad happens in our life, we blame Him. The One that we should be running to for our comfort is the One we push furthest away in our time of need.

As if Job hadn't lost enough in his life, Satan goes back to God, and God once again asks him if he has considered His servant Job. God still boasts of Job to Satan as a "blameless and upright man, one who fears God and shuns evil." A man "still holding fast to his integrity, although you incited me against him, to destroy him without cause" (Job 2:3). I find it interesting that God says Satan "incited Him against Job, to destroy Job without cause"? We want to place blame for suffering on sin or disobedience—we need to have a reason—but God allowed Job to suffer greatly even as a blameless man. Satan still does not believe that Job is as good as God thinks he is, for his next statement is, "Skin for Skin! Yes, all that a man has he will give for his life. But stretch out Your hand now and touch his bone and his flesh, and he will surely curse You to Your face!" (Job 2:4-5). The Lord told him Job was in Satan's hand but he could not kill him. "So Satan went out from the presence of the LORD, and struck Job with painful boils from the sole of his foot to the crown of his head" (Job 2:7).

This was the final straw for Job's wife. "Then his wife said to him, "Do you still hold fast to your integrity? Curse God and die!" But he said to her, "'You speak as one of the foolish women speaks. Shall we indeed accept good from God, and shall we not accept adversity?' In all this Job did not sin with his lips" (Job 2:9-10).

When life is going according to our plans, things work out how we expect them to, and we have peace and comfort all around us, it is easy to accept that God is good. But when adversity comes, when the shaking happens and we aren't so comfortable, do we hold fast to our integrity? Can we accept adversity when it comes, or do we curse God with our lips? Job's wife had had enough. She was walking through the suffering, too. She lost her home and her children, and she was watching the pain her husband was enduring. That can be a very difficult situation for a wife to be in; women like to protect their husbands—even from the hand of God. I have had to watch my husband grow in his relationship with the Lord, and that has meant watching him walk through difficult situations and circumstances. God has done a work in his mind and heart just as He has in mine. Why do we feel we need to protect them from that? I once had a conversation with a young wife who was carrying an offense for her husband. The burden of the offense was not hers to carry. He was being stretched and challenged by the Lord, and she did not like the suffering he was going through and was, quite frankly, mad. As women we must be careful that we do not encourage our husbands, or our friends, to "curse God and die!" They need us to be there for them in a time of suffering, but we must be careful of our words. Job's friends learned this truth when they did what good friends should do when they see someone they love suffer. They came to visit.

The Bible says that they "made an appointment together to come and mourn with him, and to comfort him" (verse 11).

> And when they raised their eyes from afar, and did not recognize him, they lifted their voices and wept; and each one tore his robe and sprinkled dust on his head toward heaven. So they sat down with him on the ground seven days and seven nights, and no one spoke a word to him, for they saw that his grief was very great.
>
> Job 2:12-13

When we are in the middle of suffering, it is good to have friends around us. I love that Job's friends came to him to comfort and mourn with him. In our time of suffering we need friends to gather around us to comfort and mourn with us. Their pain was great when they saw Job and they lifted their voices and wept, and then they all sat in silence for seven days. It can be very hard when you walk through a painful situation with a friend to keep silent. I know that when I have watched my friends suffer, I have wanted to somehow "fix" it for them. We want to say and do the right thing. We want to speak the words that can make it all better, but words will not always make things better. I have used words to try and help when in reality; silence sometimes is all that is needed. Words can get you into trouble. That's what happened next with Job's buddies. In trying to understand why this was happening to Job they spoke, and once they began speaking, accusations, criticism, and sin began to pour out.

Job was the first to speak, and when he did he began to curse the day he was born (Job 3:1). The Nelson King James Study Bible states that:

> Job's wish that he had never been born because his life was full of sorrow reflects a serious misunderstanding about the basic meaning of human existence. The Bible teaches that the purpose of life is not happiness but the praise of God's glory.
>
> Ephesians 1:3-14 (Nelson's NKJV Study Bible, 1997)

Remember our letter P? Reading that scripture reminded me of what my true purpose is during my time here on earth. I am here to glorify God. It is easy to live my life every day forgetting that I was not put here on earth to serve myself or worry about my own happiness but rather to love God and serve Him and bring glory and honor to His name—not my own. "Help us, O God of our salvation, for the glory of Your name; and deliver us, and provide atonement for our sins, For Your name's sake" (Psalms 79:9)! God's desire is for us to be happy, and He promised us blessings, but we've been misinformed if we believe our happiness is contingent on anything other than God. After Job speaks and cries out in sorrow, his friends begin to offer their "comfort" and "advice." After all, that's what friends are for. The first to speak is Eliphaz, and from his understanding there can be no other explanation than that Job has sinned. In Job 4:8, he states, "Even as I have seen, those who plow iniquity and sow trouble reap the same." Then he continues in chapter five with his belief that God is chastening Job. In verse 17 he says, "Happy is the man whom God corrects, therefore do not despise the chastening of the Almighty." While there is truth to the fact that the Lord does correct us, and we should not despise His correction, Job's friend was making assumptions. Haven't we all done the same from time to time? We have a need to know the reasons why things are happening to us. That's why our first reaction to any type of tragedy is usually in the form of a question; "Why?" Why did God allow this, and why is God doing this to us? "Why, God, why?" That's what Job's friends attempted to answer as Job tried to make sense of everything that was happening to him. From where Job sat he had been doing life great. He was prosperous and loved God. He even made sacrifices regularly on behalf of his children just in case they had sinned against God (Job 1:5). It would seem then that suffering shouldn't happen to him, right? If only there were never any suffering Christians, but that's not how it works. God does not ask us to *understand* Him or His ways; He asks that we *obey* Him.

In March of 2007 one of our closest friends was killed in a car accident. The shock and sorrow of his death was felt by many people who loved and respected him, but watching his wife become a widow and his children lose their beloved father was excruciating. The pain and sorrow was great in our community over his death. People were wondering, "Why would God allow this?" and we struggled in our time of grief. And while we will never fully understand the reasons behind the question *why*, we can know that in His wisdom God knows our needs, and He knows how to meet us in our suffering. God understood Job, and I believe He knew that He could trust that Job could endure the suffering. We may read the story and never be able to understand the fullness of all God did at the time, but we can understand that God does not bring pain upon us to harm us, but He does allow it to make us better if we let Him. We can become bitter or allow Him to make us better; the choice really is ours.

Reading on, we discover that one friend thinks Job is to blame for his situation. The other, Bildad, believes his children are. Job's third friend to speak offers his counsel to his friend to repent. Zophar wanted Job to understand that it was unwise to question God and challenge the Lord as Job was doing. Job felt God was being unfair with him and he was honest when he spoke. "For He attacks me with a storm and repeatedly wounds me without cause. He will not let me catch my breath, but fills me instead with bitter sorrows" (Job 9:17-18). When we find ourselves in painful situations that we do not understand it can be relatively easy to make statements based on the intense feelings at the moment.

I have allowed myself to overreact with my words because of the pain I was in. Job was no different. He found himself saying things to God and questioning Him throughout his suffering. Is that wrong? I do not believe we are wrong asking God to show Himself through our suffering. When we lost our friend his wife wanted to understand why God gave marriage if we were only going to suffer the loss of our spouse. After seeking the Lord in prayer for the answer, He showed us both, on the same day, that when He created the world it was good. Unfortunately, when sin came into the world through Adam and Eve's disobedience, death was ushered in. Now we all will suffer death, decay, and loss because of sin. Bad things will happen to good people, and God is good through it all.

Job finally speaks boldly to his friends and asks them to stop talking. "You, however, smear me with lies; you are worthless physicians, all of you! If only you would be altogether silent! For you, that would be wisdom" (Job 13:4-5). Oh, my dear friend, there is so much I could write within the pages of this book, but I fear I am running out of space. When our friends are suffering let's make sure we are careful that we do not pour out accusations upon them. Seek God for comfort and understanding. He is the God of all comfort according to 1 Corinthians 1:3-4, which says,

> Blessed be the God and Father of our Lord Jesus Christ, the Father of mercies and God of all comfort, who comforts us in all our tribulation, that we may be able to comfort those who are in any trouble, with the comfort with which we ourselves are comforted by God.

For now, we will turn the pages to the end of the story, and we will see that the Lord has some questions and advice of His own to offer Job and his friends. Just as Job throughout the course of this storm asked for an explanation from God, God, too, would ask Job if he could explain some things.

> Then the Lord answered Job out of the whirlwind, and said: "Who is this who darkens counsel, by words without knowledge? Now prepare yourself like a man; I will question you, and you shall answer Me. "Where were you when I laid the foundations of the earth? Tell Me, if you have understanding.

> Job 38:1-4

The word *darken* is translated from the Hebrew word *chashak,* and it can be translated to "confuse," and the word *counsel* is the Hebrew word `*etsah* and can be translated to "purpose," so we can read verse one to say, "Who is this who confuses (my) purpose by words without "da`ath" (knowledge, understanding, wisdom)." God is not quite done. "God then confronted Job directly, 'Now what do you have to say for yourself? Are you going to haul me, the Mighty One, into court and press charges?'" (Job 40:1-2, The Message), and then Job had a new revelation.

Job answered, "I'm speechless, in awe—words fail me. I should never have opened my mouth! I've talked too much, way too much. I'm ready to shut up and listen" (Job 40:3-5, The Message). Job 40 continues with God asking Job more pointed questions.

> God addressed Job next from the eye of the storm and this is what He said: "I have some more questions for you, and I want straight answers. Do you presume to tell me what I'm doing wrong? Are you calling me a sinner so you can be a saint?"
>
> (Job 40:6-8, The Message)

When God had finished speaking,

> Job answered God: "I'm convinced: You can do anything and everything. Nothing and no one can upset your plans. You asked, 'Who is this muddying the water, ignorantly confusing the issue, second-guessing my purposes? I admit it. I was the one. I babbled on about things far beyond me, made small talk about wonders way over my head. You told me, 'Listen, and let me do the talking. Let me ask the questions. You give the answers. I admit I once lived by rumors of you; now I have it all firsthand—from my own eyes and ears! I'm sorry—forgive me. I'll never do that

again, I promise! I'll never again live on crusts of hearsay, crumbs of rumor."

Job 42:1-6 (The Message)

What a powerful story we have right at our fingertips to help us when we are suffering. At one point Job felt as though he would never see hope again (Job 7:7). Maybe you can relate to Job in that place of feeling hopeless. How have you suffered? How are you suffering now? There are many ways in which we can suffer: through the loss of a loved one, a dream, a marriage, a job, even loss of self. Some people suffer in their minds from guilt and shame of the past. Do you have wounds that cause you to turn away from God and to other vices for your comfort? Is there a wound in your heart that you carry with you every day that you believe nothing could ever make it better? Maybe you have tried to express yourself but have felt as though it would be impossible for someone to understand. There is One who does understand far better than we understand ourselves. Jesus is His name, and this is what we have in Him.

> We have a great high priest, who has gone into heaven, and He is Jesus the Son of God. That is why we must hold on to what we have said about him. Jesus understands every weakness of ours, because he was tempted in every way that we are. But he did not sin! So whenever we are in need, we should come bravely before the throne of our merciful God. There we will be treated with undeserved kindness, and we will find help.
>
> Hebrews 4:14-16 (CEV)

Jesus suffered in every way so we would never be able to say, "He does not understand." I do not know where your pain lies, and sometimes I have a hard time expressing my own. I do know Jesus understands everything about each one of us. He knows our pain, and He wants to help us understand how to overcome the battle that wants to make us believe we are hopeless. Beloved, run into the arms of Jesus to find the comfort and understanding you need and allow Him to cover your wound with His bandage of healing. Remember, nothing to Him is trivial; it all matters. *You* matter.

Questions to consider:

1) Can you relate to Job? If so, how?

2) Where does Job 32:8 tell us our understanding comes from?

3) Do you stuff your emotion, or are you able to express yourself?

4) What can we learn about God from Job 36:26?

5) What kind of counsel should we seek according to Proverbs 1:5 in the New King James Version?

6) How honest do you believe one should be when speaking to God?

7) What mistakes did Job's friends make, if any? Have you made similar ones?

8) Job had one more friend offer advice; his name was Elihu. What three specific reasons does he say God causes the storms for Job 37:13?

9) Read Job 42. What did God say to Job's friends Eliphaz, Bildad, and Zophar?

10) Continuing in Job 42, what did the Lord do to Job and what did Job do for his friends? (verse10)

11) Read James 1:2-4. What does verse two tell us we are to do?

12) What does the testing of our faith produce?

13) What are we to let patience have? For what reason?

14) Read James 5:11. What can we learn from this verse?

15) What does James 5:13 tell us we should do if we are suffering?

# V Is for Victorious

## God Says I am *Victorious*

For whatever is born of God is *victorious* over the world; and this is the victory that conquers the world, even our faith. Who is it that is *victorious* over [that conquers] the world but he who believes that Jesus is the Son of God [who adheres to, trusts in, and relies on that fact]?

1 John 5:4-5 (Amplified Bible)

*Victorious:* having achieved a victory; conquering; triumphant (dictionary.com, LLC, 2011).

Several years ago I was asked by a local school if I would work as a one-on-one aide for a student who had difficulty making good decisions. He was a great kid who just could not, or would not, follow the rules. He was constantly spoken to by his teachers, sent to the principal, and quite frequently suspended both in school and out. As I began working with him and I got to know him, I began to see him far differently than those who saw him as a troublemaker and a "bad kid." I started to see a young man who needed to know he was able to make better choices. I saw a young man who needed to know that not everyone had given up on him. So many people in his life had grown weary and did not know how to handle him any more. He had been given up by his birth mother and placed in foster care. He moved from different foster homes and then was adopted, but his adoptive parents could not handle his rebellion and in their weariness had all but given up on him. I could see he was full of anger and resentment, but what I also saw was a desire for someone to have his back. He longed for someone to help show him what the better options were. He really wanted to find someone who would love him, accept him, and teach him.

One morning, as we were sitting on the bus together, he began to talk about his future with me. We discussed what life could possibly hold for him. I remember asking him what he wanted to be doing in five years. His answer was that he hoped he wasn't in jail. Oh, how my heart broke for him and the other students I have met throughout the years who have voiced the same desire. I looked at him and said, "You know, if you always do what you've always done, you will always get what you've always gotten." Now, I cannot take credit for the quote, nor can I give credit to whom credit is due. I really don't know. Someone once shared that quote with me, and it changed my life. It was time for him to see that if he wanted to stay out of jail and turn his life around, then he had to stop doing what he had always done and begin to try a new approach to life. It was time for him to put away the actions that were always causing him trouble and learn to respond differently to situations in life. I can relate to that, can't you? Have you ever responded to situations in your life and discovered that maybe, just maybe, you needed a "time out" for incorrect behavior? I know I have—far too many times actually—and I have learned through the loving correction of a merciful, heavenly Father that if "I always do what I've always done, I will always get what I've always gotten." The areas in my life I so desperately need to see a change in will stay the same and if they stay the same, so will every other aspect of my life. The Bible is my connection, my source of information that allows me to know God's character and ways. I know that He wants far more for me, for us, than a life full of despair and defeat. His Word is full of good promises for us.

He has already enabled us, by His Holy Spirit, to live victorious lives—lives that are able to overcome the battles we walk through.

It was no different for His chosen people, the Israelites, when they were living as slaves to the Egyptians. God didn't want them living as slaves in Egypt; He wanted them set apart for Him and He had a plan to make it happen. Unfortunately for the Israelites, however, while they saw God do incredible miracles to get them out of Egypt, they could never fully leave Egypt. It was always in the back of their minds that somehow it would be better to go back to the place where they came from. Whenever life got tough out in the desert they begged to go back to Egypt to the life of a slave. Aren't we like that at times? When we become uncomfortable waiting for the Promised Land to come, it's easy to decide life was easier back in Egypt. We decide to go back to the familiar thing rather than move on to the place that is unknown to us. Why? Because in the familiar we are comfortable. It's less scary than something completely new to us even though the familiar may be the unhealthiest place for us to be. When the Israelites stood at the Red Sea and realized that Pharaoh was chasing them, fear took over. Exodus 14:10 tells us, "As Pharaoh drew near, the sons of Israel looked, and behold, the Egyptians were marching after them, and they became very frightened; so the sons of Israel cried out to the Lord" (NAS).

This was their cry,

> Then they said to Moses, "Is it because there were no graves in Egypt that you have taken us away to die in the wilderness? Why have you dealt with us in this way, bringing us out of Egypt? Is this not the word that we spoke to you in Egypt, saying, 'Leave us alone that we may serve the Egyptians'? For it would have been better for us to serve the Egyptians than to die in the wilderness.
>
> Exodus 14:11-12 (NAS)

Now, fear itself is not a sin, and I don't blame them for having fear at seeing the Egyptians marching toward them with the sea behind them. It seemed as though there was no place to escape. But did they really tell Moses to leave them alone so they could continue as slaves? While there are those who would rather continue to be a slave to their victim mindset, I believe most of us have a desire for change. And in order to see that change we are going to need to follow the Lord's commands. While the Egyptians are moving closer to the Israelites,

> Moses said to the people; "Do not fear! Stand by and see the salvation of the Lord which He will accomplish for you today; for the Egyptians whom you have seen today, you will never see them again forever. The Lord will fight for you while you keep silent.
>
> Exodus 14:13-14 (NAS)

God spoke such a powerful message through Moses that day when He said, "Stand by and see…" That's the same message He has spoken to me throughout the years when I have wanted to turn and run back to familiarity even if it hasn't been the best place for me. We must stop running back. We must learn to stand by and see…to watch…to wait…to see what the Lord can and will accomplish for us. His desire for us is to know that never again will we see those Egyptians hunting us down. What a promise of hope and victory that statement is to me. How was the Lord fighting for them? In their silence. And how are we supposed to behave while the Lord fights for us? Remain silent. That alone is one of the biggest areas in my life I needed to have a victory in. I needed to learn how to remain silent in the battle, remembering that the Lord has a battle plan for my victory. I needed to learn how to let go of the grumbling and complaining over the situation I was in, learning how to speak the Word over it and allowing God to show me how He would bring about the victory. The trouble is we have become so accustomed to looking at our problems we forget to look to Him as our Help, our Strength, and our Source of Wisdom to get us through the problem. We become victims to our problems rather than victorious over our problems. How do we know if we are a victim? If, year after year, we rehash the betrayal in a marriage that caused it to fail, or if we continually focus on how others have wronged us refusing to allow forgiveness, we are victims. If I allow the pain of the past to consume all of my todays and tomorrows, I am a victim. When we refuse to humble ourselves and offer an apology that may lead to reconciliation in a broken relationship, we become the victim. A victim of our own pride. We are a victim when we refuse to listen to the counsel or advice that can help move us forward towards victory but instead choose to continue in our old habits. Do you know someone who, when you are trying to help them see a situation differently, resorts to, "I know, but..." and then they proceed to tell why they have a right to feel the way they do? When we use *but* to explain why we have the right to be a victim we will stay the victim. The story never changes, and our focus remains the same.

Well, God says, "Let me fight for you. You just remain silent. Watch me work on your behalf!" How can we expect to have a victory over a situation if we are always talking with negativity and believe that it can never change? God has a different approach. Stop talking. It's okay to use your past as a place of reference, but God never intended for it to become a place of residence. There does come a time when we have to let things go because God wants us to move forward, always growing and changing and not standing still.

"Then the Lord said to Moses, "Why are you crying out to me? Tell the sons of Israel to go forward" (Exodus 14:15, NAS). I love that verse. The Lord asks, "Why are you crying out to me?" as if to say, "Don't just stand there and cry. Do something!" It reminds me of the story in the New Testament of the invalid man at the Pool of Bethesda.

Now there is in Jerusalem a pool near the Sheep Gate. This pool in the Hebrew is called Bethesda, having five porches (alcoves, colonnades, doorways). In these lay a great number of sick folk—some blind, some crippled, and some paralyzed (shriveled up)—waiting for the bubbling up of the water. For an angel of the Lord went down at appointed seasons into the pool and moved and stirred up the water; whoever then first, after the stirring up of the water, stepped in was cured of whatever disease with which he was afflicted. There was a certain man there who had suffered with a deep-seated and lingering disorder for thirty-eight years. When Jesus noticed him lying there [helpless], knowing that he had already been a long time in that condition, He said to him, 'Do you want to become well? [Are you really in earnest about getting well?]' The invalid answered, Sir, I have nobody when the water is moving to put me into the pool; but while I am trying to come [into it] myself, somebody else steps down ahead of me. Jesus said to him, Get up! Pick up your bed (sleeping pad) and walk! Instantly the man became well and recovered his strength and picked up his bed and walked.

John 5:2-9a (Amplified Bible)

Did you notice that Jesus didn't throw the man a pity party? He didn't tell him how sorry He was for his thirty-eight years of suffering or how horrible it was that no one would help him. Sometimes we need to ask ourselves if we *really, truly, earnestly* want to have victory in our lives. Do we truly want change in our lives, or are we so comfortable in our defeat that we won't just get up and walk? The man blamed his condition on the fact that no one would carry him to the waters. Sometimes God will use people to help carry us to the waters of victory, but there comes a time when we must rely on God and our own determination to get there.

Exodus 17 is a great example for us as it shows us how God uses others to help us obtain victory in the battles we face. Once again we go back to the Israelites in the desert.

> So Joshua fought the Amalekites as Moses had ordered, and Moses, Aaron and Hur went to the top of the hill. As long as Moses held up his hands, the Israelites were winning, but whenever he lowered his hands, the Amalekites were winning. When Moses' hands grew tired, they took a stone and put it under him and he sat on it. Aaron and Hur held his hands up—one on one side, one on the other—so that his hands remained steady till sunset. So Joshua overcame the Amalekite army with the sword.
>
> Exodus 17:10-13 (NIV)

Battles are hard, and victories don't come easily. There are times when we need the support of others to help us defeat our attacker and become victorious. James 5:16 says we are to, "Therefore, confess your sins to one another, and pray for one another so that you may be healed. The effective prayer of a righteous man can accomplish much" (James 5:16, NASV). Just like Moses needed Aaron and Hur to help lift his arms, I have needed good, solid, Christian friends to come beside me and help lift my arms. There have been times when the battle seemed far too great to win and victory seemed far out of reach. I could not have overcome the battle that was raging within me without the accountability of those the Lord brought into my life to help hold me up. As I confessed, they prayed and lifted my arms for me, and then victory came. Allow God to bring others into your life to help lift your arms if you are weary in the battle. Be honest with them, confess to them the depth of the situation, and allow them to bring you godly wisdom and counsel. Don't be afraid of God's truth.

Walter Anderson said, "Our lives improve only when we take chances—and the first and most difficult risk we can take is to be honest with ourselves." Allow God to use others to speak truth in your life to help you grow and mature. Desire to be the person God designed you to be. Become a good listener! God gave us two ears and one mouth so we could hear twice as much as we speak! We may say we want change in our lives but the fruit of that only comes when we put to practice what the Lord directs us to do. James 1:22 reminds us that we are to be, "doers of the word, and not hearers only, deceiving yourselves."

We must be careful to not allow ourselves to become victims on the way to becoming victorious. When the Israelites were challenged in any way they always turned to grumbling and threats. They always became the victims. God walks us to a victory through a course of events and circumstances that He knows will bring about the lasting changes He is looking for in us. He chose the route for the Israelites to take when they left Egypt. He knew the best path for the desired outcome.

> When Pharaoh let the people go, God did not lead them on the road through the Philistine country, though that was shorter. For God said, "If they face war, they might change their minds and return to Egypt." So God led the people around by the desert road toward the Red Sea. The Israelites went up out of Egypt armed for battle.
>
> Exodus 13:17-18 (NIV)

The Israelites lost sight of the Promised Land while on their journey to the Promised Land because they became victims along the way. We must be vigilant over our minds and not allow ourselves to be persuaded that we are victims when God turns the heat up. I have known people who were actually victims that talked as though they were victorious, and I have known others who have lived as victims when they should have seen themselves far differently.

We will all have opportunities arise when we will need to choose between being a victim or victor. We may believe that we have every right to be the victim, and that very well may be true. Many people become victims through no fault of their own. In fact, you may be one of them. Things might have happened in your life that have left you broken and victimized, and for that I am truly sorry. I know that God takes the victimization of His children very seriously. Psalm 10:14 says, "But You, O God, do see trouble and grief; You consider it to take it in hand. The victim commits himself to You; You are the helper of the fatherless" (NIV). The greatest victory you can have is when you no longer live as a victim but release your victimization over to the Lord for Him to take care of. Romans 12:19 tells us, "Beloved, never avenge yourselves, but leave the way open for [God's] wrath; for it is written, Vengeance is Mine, I will repay (requite), says the Lord" (Amplified Bible). Through Christ we really and truly can leave those who have wronged us in His hands to deal with and live free from the pain of it.

If we earnestly desire to have victory in our lives then we must come up with a battle plan. The best battle plan we have at our disposal is the Word of God. He has given us instructions and the ability to know what we must do to bring about a victory; what we must do is desire it. We must be growing in our knowledge of the Word and in our knowledge of Him. When we don't see the victory in our life right away, our first inclination is to run back. But we must remain steadfast in the battle. Do not allow the enemy to fill you with fear but march on to the victorious life God has waiting for you. We can overcome the world and live wonderful, victorious lives because we believe in Jesus Christ, and through Him we can overcome any obstacle thrown at us. Let's go out together and become victors instead of victims. Let's not live any longer believing that we have a right to live as a victim because of what was done to us. Let's live our days on earth knowing that we can overcome anything because He has enabled us through the power of the Holy Spirit to do so. Are you ready to go do battle? I am. Let's pick up our swords, the Word of God, and begin the fight right where the battle is raging in the center of our minds. We can say with boldness and confidence, "But thanks be to God, Who gives us the victory [making us conquerors] through our Lord Jesus Christ" (1 Corinthians 15:57, Amplified Bible). Hold on tight and cover your ears. I sense a victory cry coming over the horizon! Praise God! It's about time!

Questions to consider:

1) Read Deuteronomy 8:2. Why did God lead the Israelites through the wilderness for forty years?

2) What wilderness have you been led through and why?

3) Read Deuteronomy 8:6-10. What does verse six say we should do? What do the remaining verses tell us God had for His children?

4) Following the Red Sea escape, the Israelites sang a song to the Lord. Read Exodus 15. How did they describe the Lord in verse 2?

5) Continuing in Exodus 15, how many days did they travel before they began to grumble again (verse 22)? What did the Lord do in verse 25? What was the promise in verse 26?

6) Read Exodus 9:16. God says there is a specific reason He allowed the Israelites to remain in Egypt under Pharaoh's rule for a time. What was it?

7) Often times we want to find the reasons behind the whys. Read John 9:1-12. What does Jesus say in verse 3?

8) Do you believe God still desires to do the same today?

9) Read Hebrews 3:7-19. What was the reason given for the Israelites never entering the rest of God (verse 19)?

10) Read John 4:46-54. What did Jesus say people needed to see before they believed? In verse 49, what does it say the man believed?

11) Is it possible that we are looking today for signs and wonders rather than believing the Word that Jesus has spoken to us? Has this ever happened to you?

12) Read John 7:37-38. How are we to believe in Jesus? What will flow from us?

13) What do you consider to be a victory in your life when you see it happen?

14) What can you do to make sure you continue to live a victorious Christian life?

15) Will you choose to be a victim or a victor when challenged by God?

 Is for Wise

## God Says I am *Wise*

"For the Lord gives *wisdom*; from His mouth come knowledge and understanding."

Proverbs 2:6

*Wise:* having the power of discerning and judging properly as to what is true or right; possessing discernment, judgment, or discretion (dictionary.com, 2011).

*Wisdom:* the quality or state of being wise; knowledge of what is true or right coupled with just judgment as to action; sagacity, discernment, or insight (dictionary.com, 2011).

When the Lord drops a word into my heart that will go with the letter of a certain chapter, He usually reminds me of a situation in my life that will relate well to the word. As I have thought about the W word, knowing that it is going to be on wisdom, I have been somewhat apprehensive as to the situation in my life that I may have to spill. I am hoping that I can share some of the wisest decisions I have made in my life; however, I don't have many of those stories running through my mind at this moment. The ones that seem to be coming back to me are the not-so-wise moments, unfortunately. After all, it is usually in the unwise moments that we learn our valuable lessons, right?

Several years ago while I was still a very young and immature Christian, I had quite a temper. I could fly off the handle as quick as you could snap your fingers! It is an ugly, embarrassing truth, but it is the truth. I remember one instance when we were expecting company for the weekend. My grandmother was visiting for the first time. She had never flown before, and after my grandfather's death she decided that it would be the right time to experience it. So my mother made the arrangements and together they flew from Western New York to the Syracuse airport. I was very excited to have her come for a few days. But as I prepared for their arrival, I became more and more, well, stressed, shall we say, over wanting every detail of her first visit perfect. There were loads of laundry to be done, meals to prepare, groceries to be picked up, kids to be taken care of, etc., etc., etc. The list was long because I wanted everything to be "just so" for her arrival.

As I went about the day checking the finished tasks off my list, I noticed that the lawn really should be mowed. Now, my sweet husband, who had been working twelve-hour nights, was trying hard to get some sleep. I believe I had gone in once or twice and gently, I am sure it was *gently*, tried to wake him to remind him that there was a lot to be done in a few short hours. The kids were making a mess as fast as I could clean it up, and once again the lawn needed mowing. Well, he didn't get up at my command, I mean gentle request, so that was one more thing I added to my list. I eventually marched out to the garage and took matters into my own hands. That was not the wisest decision. I was mad. After all, I was the *only one* who cared about things around there! And I was the *only one* working to get things done around there! We only had a push mower at the time, and the more I walked, the more upset I became. It wasn't too long before I was stomping along, pushing that mower with such force that I must have looked ridiculous to the neighbors. I was practically running while pushing the mower. It gives me a chuckle as I remember it. I am glad I can laugh about this now because I sure wasn't laughing then. As I mowed

I came to an extension cord that ran about twenty feet across the yard to the house. I am not sure why all sense of wisdom left me at that moment, but I can see very clearly that we don't make the wisest decisions when mad. I bent over, grabbed that extension cord, (I was standing twenty feet from the outlet), and pulled it out with the force of all my anger. In amazement and horror I stood and watched as the plug of the electrical cord came back at me like a mad snake and landed right on my lower lip. I had prong marks and a nice gash in my lower lip, and my goodness, how the lip does bleed! With my hands over my mouth I ran into the house. Pat had no choice but to get up now; we needed to go to the emergency room! So now I had to add that to my list of things to accomplish before the plane arrived. I actually couldn't get the stitches in my lip before her plane arrived due to the large crowd at the hospital, so I went to the airport with ice on my big fat lip, greeted Grandma and my mother, and then went back to the emergency room for four stitches. Embarrassing? Just a little. Lack of wisdom? You could say.

I really could share one story after another of times that I have used little wisdom in my decision-making and had horrible consequences because of it. If you think about it, our regrets come from decisions made that lacked wisdom on our part. Financial crises happen because we aren't wise with our money. We may lose job opportunities because we are unwise in our actions at work. We get hurt in relationships because we don't use wisdom with those we have allowed ourselves to become involved with. Our health deteriorates when we aren't using wisdom in the care of our bodies. People make unwise decisions that can cost them their marriage, relationships with their children, and even entire bank accounts. The list goes on and on; every area of our life requires us to make wise decisions if we are going to live a life full of God's blessings. We are a very *feeling*-driven society, and we base most of our decisions on how we feel about the situation at the time. We don't stop and think about the wisdom of a decision—only how "good" we think it is going to make us feel at the time. If I am not going to base my decisions on my feelings, and I want the best possible outcome of each decision, how do I begin to discover wisdom? Job asked a very good question. "From where then does wisdom come? And where *is* the place of understanding?" (Job 28:20). It goes on to say,

> Destruction and Death say, "We've heard only rumors of where wisdom can be found." God alone understands the way to wisdom; He knows where it can be found, for He looks throughout the whole earth and sees everything under the heavens. He decided how hard the winds should blow and how much rain should fall. He made the laws for the rain and laid out a path for the lightning. Then He saw wisdom and evaluated it. He set it in place and examined it thoroughly. And this is what He says to all humanity: "The fear of the Lord is true wisdom; to forsake evil is real understanding."
>
> Job 28:22-28

We can find wisdom and know how to gain a heart of understanding when we hold fast to a very important principle of the Word. True wisdom is found in the fear of the Lord, and understanding is found when we let go of sin. Oftentimes, however, we do not want to let go of our sin, and we have become so casual in our relationship with the Lord, that we no longer hold the proper fear or reverence for Him. When I began to gain more understanding of Who God was, I began to view Him more fearfully. The word *fear* is taken from the Hebrew word *yir'ah* and translates to "to revere and respect" (Blue Letter Bible, 1996-2011). To fear God is to respect and revere Him. We will walk in wisdom when we walk in the fear of the Lord. We may be faithful church attendees, we may be faithful in our tithe, but if we have no reverence for God in our daily lives, we are not wise. Living a life in fear, or reverence, for the Lord means that I am keeping Him always before me. I am very aware that He sees everything I do and my actions should be both pleasing to Him and bring Him honor. Would those around us recognize the glory of the Lord in our lives? We need to pray and ask Him if our speech, attitudes, actions, and thoughts bring Him the honor He deserves. In James 1 Paul tells us that we can go to God and ask for wisdom, and it will be given to the one who asks. "If any of you lacks wisdom, he should ask God, who gives generously to all without finding fault, and it will be given to him" (James 1:5, NIV). That is exactly what King David's son, Solomon, did when he inherited the throne from his father. He must have understood the importance of wisdom because when the Lord offered him *anything* he asked for the Lord's wisdom.

> At Gibeon the Lord appeared to Solomon in a dream by night; and God said, "Ask! What shall I give you?" And Solomon said: "You have shown great mercy to Your servant David my father, because he walked before You in truth, in righteousness, and in uprightness of heart with You; You have continued this great kindness for him, and You have given him a son to sit on his throne, as it is this day. Now, O Lord my God, You have made Your servant king instead of my father David, but I am a little child; I do not know how to go out or come in. And Your servant is in the midst of Your people whom You have chosen, a great people, too numerous to be numbered or counted. Therefore give to Your servant an understanding heart to judge Your people, that I may discern between good and evil. For who is able to judge this great people of Yours.
>
> 1 Kings 3:5-9 (NKJV)

Solomon chose to ask for a gift of far greater use than riches and honor; he asked for an understanding heart. That request pleased the Lord so much that He promised him everything else, as well. Solomon would not only have a wise and understanding heart, he would also have what he didn't ask for, riches and honor (1 Kings 3:10-13). Humility goes a long way with the Lord. Solomon's popularity increased and all the earth came to hear his wisdom, and when they came they brought him gifts, increasing his wealth. (1 Kings 10:24-25). Can you imagine? The entire earth's population wanted to sit and listen to him speak because they knew that what came from his mouth was the wisdom of God. I love to sit under a good Bible teacher; one that can teach the truth of God's Word wisely is a great gift to have.

But even with his wisdom, Solomon had a weakness, and that weakness was women. In 1 Kings we discover that Solomon created quite a little harem for himself, which goes against everything God had spoken to him.

> And he had seven hundred wives, princesses, and three hundred concubines; and his wives turned away his heart. For it was so, when Solomon was old, that his wives turned his heart after other gods; and his heart was not loyal to the Lord his God, as was the heart of his father David.
>
> 1 Kings 11:3-4 (NKJV)

Solomon's lack of control over his desire for women cost him the Kingdom.

> So the Lord became angry with Solomon, because his heart had turned from the Lord God of Israel, who had appeared to him twice, and had commanded him concerning this thing, that he should not go after other gods; but he did not keep what the Lord had commanded. Therefore the

Lord said to Solomon, "Because you have done this, and
have not kept My covenant and My statutes, which I have
commanded you, I will surely tear the kingdom away from
you and give it to your servant."

1 Kings 11:9-11 (NKJV)

God had given Solomon the wisdom that no man had ever
possessed before, yet he allowed his desire for women to overrule
his obedience to the Lord. Have we allowed our own desires to
ever overrule our obedience to the Lord? Sure we have. Every time
we allow the fear of the Lord to diminish from sight. What have
we lost when we haven't controlled ourselves and we've disobeyed
God? Solomon lost his kingdom. What was your kingdom? Have
you lost your kingdom because desire overruled wisdom? If so,
what was it? A marriage lost because of unfaithfulness? Did you
lose your health due to alcoholism, drug abuse or gluttony? Your
savings and possessions from a gambling addiction? Have you
forfeited a relationship with a close friend or family member
because pride won't allow an apology? We can lose our jobs, our
homes, even our own lives when we fail to walk in wisdom. I have
allowed myself to make many foolish decisions because I didn't
want to wait on the Lord. I have either spoken a word too soon
that caused a hurt or brought an offense to someone. Or I have
spent money foolishly on items I didn't need or ideas I thought
were going to be great investments. I have asked the Lord to
forgive me for the many times I ignored His counsel and wisdom
and moved forward doing my own thing. I am working now to get
myself free from the consequences of bad decisions, but I know
that He forgives, and He uses everything for His glory; nothing
is ever wasted with God. But I don't want to lose kingdoms that
He has intended for me to have. I wonder if Proverbs 3:5-8 came
out of this experience for Solomon.

Trust in the Lord with all your heart and lean not on your own understanding; in all your ways acknowledge Him, and He will make your paths straight. Do not be wise in your own eyes; fear the Lord and shun evil. This will bring health to your body and nourishment to your bones. Proverbs 3:5-8 (NIV)

Do you think Solomon realized that he had been "wise in his own eyes" and wanted us to learn from his mistakes? We can capture the wisdom of Solomon's heart for ourselves through reading the book of Proverbs. He begins chapter one by letting us know that they were written for a purpose. That purpose was to help us in…

… attaining wisdom and discipline; for understanding words of insight; for acquiring a disciplined and prudent life, doing what is right and just and fair; for giving prudence to the simple, knowledge and discretion to the young- let the wise listen and add to their learning, and let the discerning get guidance-for understanding proverbs and parables, the sayings and riddles of the wise. Proverbs 1: 2-6 (NIV, 1984)

Solomon goes on to tell us in Proverbs 4,

Do not forsake wisdom, and she will protect you; love her, and she will watch over you. Wisdom is supreme; therefore get wisdom. Though it cost all you have, get understanding. Esteem her, and she will exalt you; embrace her, and she will honor you. She will set a garland of grace on your head and present you with a crown of splendor.

Proverbs 4:6-9

We have God's wisdom available to us as we pray and request it, but like Solomon we must put it into action, or it will cost us. I am so thankful to have prayed many years ago, after reading James 1:5, asking God to give me His wisdom just as He gave it to Solomon. More than anything, I want to be protected in my walk with Him by obtaining wisdom. I desperately wanted to know that I could make wise decisions based upon His wisdom and not my own. Since the day that I began to pray for it, the choice has always been up to me as to whether or not I would follow the voice of wisdom or my own foolish desires. If you have not prayed for God to give you wisdom in your decision-making, I encourage you to do so. Living in the days in which we do, we need to have God's wisdom and understanding to guide us and protect us. Don't be fooled into believing wisdom is found through any other source. Remember that true wisdom, the wisdom we need to help us live the full life God has for us, is found only through God. He will not share His glory with any other (Isaiah 48:11, NLT). There are many New Age practices drawing us away from God's Word into a spiritual realm we are forbidden to entertain. Practicing sorcery, divination, witchcraft and consulting with mediums and psychics arouses the Lord's anger and is considered evil in His sight (2 Chronicles 33:6). We only need to seek the Word to discover our future. Wisdom is the only adjective that we have studied thus far that requires us to ask for it. All others are given to us when we accept Christ. We are given wisdom when we sincerely ask God for it. What are you waiting for? Let the asking begin!

This is an acronym that the Lord has given to me that I have hanging on the wall of my office to help me follow His voice of wisdom from now on. I pray it helps you too.

- *W-* Wait. Don't move too fast. "The wisdom of the prudent is to give thought to their ways, but the folly of fools is deception" (Proverbs 14:8).

- *I*- Increase in knowledge of the Word, which will "make me wiser than all my enemies" (Psalm 119:98, NIV)!

- *S*- Seek the advice of godly counsel. "Pride only breeds quarrels, but wisdom is found in those who take advice" (Proverbs 13:10).

- *D*- Delight in wisdom! "A fool finds pleasure in evil conduct, but a man of understanding delights in wisdom" (Proverbs 10:23).

- *O*- Obey the voice of wisdom, which can save me from making foolish decisions. "Do not forsake wisdom, and she will protect you; love her, and she will watch over you" (Proverbs 4:6).

- *M*- Mature in understanding God's Word and His wisdom. "And Jesus grew in wisdom and stature, and in favor with God and men" (Luke 2:52).

Questions to consider:

1)  We discover in James chapter 1, that there is a stipulation for us when we ask for God's wisdom. What do we learn from reading verse 6?

2)  What does verse 7 tell us?

3)  Read 1 Kings 11:1-2. Why did the Lord forbid intermarriage? What does verse 2 tell us about Solomon?

4)  What did God promise Solomon in verses 12 and 13?

5) Proverbs 1 explains the consequences of rejecting God's wisdom. What can we learn from verses 20 through 33?

6) What are the moral benefits to finding wisdom as described in Proverbs 2?

7) What does Proverbs 24:3 tell us? What do you think this means?

8) Read 1 Corinthians 1:19-30. What does verse 20 say? What does verse 25 say?

9) Read 1 Corinthians 2:12-14. What have we received according to verse 12? According to verse 13, what do we speak? Can the man without the Spirit of God accept the things of the Spirit, i.e. God's wisdom?

10) How does James 3:17 describe God's wisdom?

11) Can you recognize times when you have allowed your natural wisdom to overrule God's wisdom in your decision making?

12) Do you have a story you are willing to share about a decision that might not have been the wisest one to make?

13) Ephesians 1:16-19 gives us a wonderful prayer to follow as we lift one another up to the Lord. How does it encourage you to pray?

# X Is for Excluded

## God Says I am *Excluded*

"Blessed are you when men hate you, and when they *exclude* you, and revile you, and cast out your name as evil, For the Son of Man's sake."

Luke 6:22

*Excluded:* to shut or keep out; prevent the entrance of, to expel and keep out; thrust out; eject (dictionary.com, 2011).

*Blessed:* divinely or supremely favored; fortunate (dictionary.com, 2011).

I'm not sure if you wondered if I might find a word that begins with the letter X or not, but I didn't. Well, actually I did; it was Xerses, and that wasn't going to work. So I did the next best thing and chose to get a little creative with the letter *x*. After praying about it, I felt the Lord was leading me to study the word exclude. I was sure I must be wrong; after all, being excluded doesn't sound very uplifting or encouraging, does it? What did He want us to know and understand about this word? When I think about all the words we have done throughout this study, they all make me want to stand up and scream, "Yes! I am accepted, beautiful, holy, etc.!" But to stand up and scream, "Yes! I am excluded!"—that might not happen quite as quickly as I would like it to, especially with the sanguine personality I have inherited. Sanguines like being the life of the party. When I studied the Word to gain clarity, I began to see a common thread within the Old and New Testaments of those who have walked the road of Christianity before us. They were excluded.

The more I learn about the Prophets throughout the Old Testament; the more I understand exclusion. These were individuals who God called to speak His Words to a nation who didn't always want to hear what God had to say. There were often times when the message of the Lord was a demand for repentance and a call to turn away from sin. When Jezebel became Queen she destroyed all but 100 of the Lord's prophets and placed around her prophets of false gods. She was determined to kill Elijah, the Prophet of God, because he challenged the lies of her false prophets with the truth of the One True God (1 Kings 18 & 19). Prophets of the Old Testament, like Jeremiah, those who were faithful to speak the truth of God's coming judgment, were probably not the first names written on the guest list for the next big social event of the season. I have so much respect for the Prophets because they spoke, with no apologies, the words God wanted His people to hear.

Jesus also understood exclusion; after all, He didn't get many invitations to the Pharisees and Sadducees gatherings, did He? Once He began to challenge them in their teachings and their understanding of God, the meetings they had together became more *about* Him and how they could get *rid* of Him. They weren't interested in becoming friends with this guy who was stirring up so much trouble. He really pushed their buttons. He was excluded from the "Religious Leader Club" because He wasn't afraid to challenge the people living around Him with the *truth*. There is much to be learned by reading about the life of Jesus while He was here on earth. He knew the truth because He *was* the Truth and He freely shared it with everyone regardless of how He might be perceived or viewed by them. He didn't mind stepping on a few toes here and there along the way, either. He just lived life His way, knowing what His purpose was and not worrying what people thought of Him. He spent His time doing the work of the Father regardless of how others assumed He should be spending His time. He had His priorities in order and following the crowd of the day was never important to Him. However, helping the crowd was. Jesus reached out to those who were broken, He called the children to come to Him and He took the time to sit among those whom the Religious Leaders looked down upon for being "sinners". How can we follow the example of Jesus and reach out to those around us who have become broken? James 1:27 says, "Pure and undefiled religion before God and the Father is this: to visit orphans and widows in their trouble, and to keep oneself unspotted from the world." Is our religion pure and undefiled? When we encounter the helpless, the homeless and the hopeless do we exclude them or do we include them by sharing the love Jesus has for them, and the hope of His salvation?

Jesus was able to show us, by His example, how we can live in the world and not be part of the world. He wasn't worried if His comments didn't make Him the most popular guy in the crowd. I love that He knew that it would be a challenge for us to live in this world and not become part of it, so He prayed for us. In John 17, Jesus prayed to His Father for His disciples and, *guess what?*, we are included in that prayer. "I do not pray that You should take them out of the world, but that You should keep them from the evil one. They are not of the world, just as I am not of the world. Sanctify them by Your truth. Your word is truth" (John 17:15-17).

Jesus didn't ask God to remove all of His disciples and place them in the "All Inclusive Club for Christ." Rather, He prayed that God would keep us from the evil one. Jesus understood the trials that we will endure while living in this world, He also understood that Satan is "the ruler of this world" (John 14:31), so He prays for us to be guarded from the evil one. Why must we be guarded against him? Because he is the Father of lies (John 8:44) and has been twisting God's Word in this world since the beginning of time.

*The Berenstain Bears and the Truth* (Berenstain, 1983) has a great poem on the inside front cover. It reads, "No matter how much you hope, no matter how you try, you can't make truth out of a lie." As I gaze upon our world and the moral/value system that grows further and further away from God's values, I cannot help but think of the truth that comes from the Berenstain's poem. In the book of Judges we read about a time in Israel's history when there was no king and everyone did what was right in their own eyes. We may not want to acknowledge it, but we live in a world that has slipped so far away from the principles that God intended for us to live, that we now strive to get truth out of lies, doing what is right in our own eyes. Most nights I watch the news with such great sadness in my heart as people protest and demand rights to live in ways that are far from what God ever intended for us to live. The reality of it is that you can hope and you can try, but you cannot get truth out of a lie. Unfortunately, that is not a message many want to hear and when challenged with the truth of the Word- it can become very ugly. In recent months there has been more and more criticism of anyone who takes a stand for Christ and the Bible, as the Inerrant Word of God. I came to the realization that if I were to be seen by someone faltering in my faith and caught in an act contrary to the Word, I would quickly be labeled a hypocrite. However, if I speak the Words of Christ and commit to live my life, as best as I can, according to the Word, then I run the risk of being labeled a bigot. Honestly, it is no easy task for Christians to live in a world that is opposed to Christ, and while Satan has his time to rule here on earth, the earth is going to be opposed to Christ and all who follow Him. While we may fear exclusion we must remember that Satan's club is not the one we want a membership in.

We are told that we are blessed when people look at you and hate you—when they exclude you. I have always been one to hate being excluded. I am one that hates missing anything and because of that there have been times when I have taken exclusion very personally and allowed it to depress me. It was hard to overcome the desire I had to be included in activities, with influences that were not going to bring out the best of God in me. Whenever I struggle with being excluded the first sentence of Psalm 46:10 often enters my mind. It reminds me to be still and know that He is God.

Over the last few years I have come to realize that I want God's blessing more than I want to be included in studies that spread gossip as prayer requests and social activities that are labeled as fellowship yet cause harm to our witness. I want Him to pour out His blessings upon my life and my family's and one day as He opened my eyes to the words, "blessed is the man" within the scriptures the instructions became clear. In the very first chapter of Psalms, the very first verse we read, "Blessed is the man who walks not in the counsel of the ungodly"(Psalm 1:1). I could follow Jezebel's example and surround myself with "false prophets", or people who never speak a word of God's truth in my life, or I can accept that blessing comes to me when I am no longer surrounded with ungodly counsel.

Another blessing is found in Psalm 34:8 which says, "Oh taste and see that the Lord is good; blessed is the man who trusts in Him." If I desire a blessed life, I am going to trust in the Lord and learn to put my doubts and fears to rest in His arms. I have tasted and seen the goodness of the Lord, even during moments of uncertainty. Psalm 112:1 says, "Praise the Lord! Blessed is the man who fears the Lord, Who delights greatly in His commandments." We just talked about wisdom that comes when we fear the Lord. A blessed life is a life that has the right fear, or reverence, in the Lord.

James 1:12 says, "Blessed is the man who endures temptation; for when he has been approved, he will receive the crown of life which the Lord has promised to those who love Him." Oh, temptation is sure to come and it can truly be a battle, but it does not need to win in our lives. We can overcome the lure of the tempter because Jesus made it possible. We can have victory over sin, over the temptations that come our way and over the devil. First Peter 5:8 is a good scripture to be mindful of as we are told to "be self-controlled and alert. Your enemy the devil prowls around like a roaring lion looking for someone to devour." Do you know what I noticed when I read this verse? In every translation it reads the devil prowls around *like* or *as* a roaring lion. Not one translation told me that he *is* a roaring lion. Is he powerful? Yes he is, but do believers have the authority to strip him of his power? You bet we do. Not one single time in the New Testament is the church ever told to pray for God the Father, or Jesus, to do anything against the devil. The believer has been given the authority to confront the devil. Look at Ephesians 6 and follow the instructions. We are told to, "Put on all of God's armor so that you will be able to stand firm against all strategies of the devil" (Ephesians 6:11, NLT). Yes, he has strategies and he has schemes, but God has given us every spiritual blessing to overcome and defeat any of the enemy's schemes.

And lastly, Psalm 94:12, "Blessed is the man whom You instruct, O Lord, and teach out of Your law." Please allow the Lord to instruct and teach you. Allow Him to exclude you from people, places and things that will cause temptations to rise up that may bring you down. Push your pride aside and if He begins to show you that it is time to remove yourself from extra-curricular activities that have a negative influence upon you, follow Him. Run for the exit door. Listen for the Prophets who are speaking the truth of His Word. This isn't a popularity contest.

Questions to consider:

1)  How do you endure exclusion?

2)  What would you say the world accepts as truths but is actually lies according to the Word of God?

3)  Would you agree that the world views Christians as hypocrites and bigots? Why or why not?

4)  What does 2 Corinthians 4: 3-4 tell us has happened to "those who are perishing"?

5)  Have you ever been excluded because of your faith?

6)  What does 1 John 5:19 tell us? What do you believe this means?

7)  Have you, at this point in your life, learned how to include those who are looked down upon by others?

8)  Read Isaiah 61:1-3. According to these verses what are we called to?

9)  How does Jesus describe the devil in John 8:44? In contrast, what does John 8:31-32 say?

10)  How do you live in this world but show that you are not of it? What makes you different?

# Y IS FOR YOKED

## God Says I am *Yoked* with Jesus

Come to Me, all you who labor and are heavy-laden and overburdened, and I will cause you to rest. [I will ease and relieve and refresh your souls.] Take My *yoke* upon you and learn of Me, for I am gentle (meek) and humble (lowly) in heart, and you will find rest (relief and ease and refreshment and recreation and blessed quiet) for your souls. For My *yoke* is wholesome (useful, good—not harsh, hard, sharp, or pressing, but comfortable, gracious, and pleasant), and My burden is light and easy to be borne.

Matthew 11:28-30 (Amplified Bible)

*Yoke*: something that couples or binds together; a bond or tie. Verb: to be or become joined, linked, or united (dictionary.com, 2011).

Well, here we are; nearly to the end of the alphabet and our quest to discover whom God says we really are in Christ through each letter. I am so thankful that He took me on this journey, and then He invited you to journey along, too. Has your view of yourself changed any? Are you able to see yourself more from God's perspective rather than your own or, more importantly, others? I know I see myself far differently than I used to. When my mind begins to wander, and I think that I am less than what

God says I am, I am far quicker these days to listen to the small voice that speaks the truth to my heart from within His Word. I am so thankful for the Word that is the very breath of God and can change anyone who really desires change. This is a lasting change that works from the inside out. As we begin to wrap up this devotional and set this season of discovery upon our bookshelves, I wondered what the Lord would want us to end with. What nugget of truth does He have for us to learn that will change how we see ourselves, and Him, for the rest of our lives? He is so good and faithful, and He will continue to teach us and guide us into all truth. We have that promise from John 16:13.

We can capture a glimpse of His desire for us to learn about Him from Jesus's statement in Matthew 11 when He said, "…Take My yoke upon you and learn of Me…" I truly want to learn of Jesus, don't you? I want to know all there is to know *about* Him so that I can be more *like* Him. I often wonder what it would have been like had I lived during His time on earth. Would I have followed Him? Would I have believed He was who He said He was, or would I have cried out with the crowd, "Crucify Him!"? I am always amazed when I think of the love and compassion He had for a people who would eventually turn on Him and nail Him to a cross. That is one of the areas that I desire to learn of Him, His heart of compassion. How was He able show compassion to the very people who would betray Him and ultimately kill Him? They were the chosen ones that should have been watching and waiting for His arrival. Yet they didn't recognize Him when He came to live among them. In the gospels, when Jesus was with multitudes of people, scripture often states that He had compassion and then tells the circumstances behind His compassion. When He saw the people, He was moved with compassion and healed sickness and disease. He was moved with compassion for the multitude who had been with Him for three days and had nothing to eat. He didn't want to send them away hungry, so with seven loaves of bread and a few fish He fed them (Matthew 15:32-39). In Mark 6:34 it says

He, "... was moved with compassion for them, because they were like sheep not having a shepherd. So He began to teach them many things." Yes, I love the compassion of Jesus. It was that very heart of compassion that saved my soul! It is His heart of compassion that sees the needs of the people and is moved to help meet them.

I'm sure that it must have been out of His heart of compassion that He spoke the words from Matthew 11:28-30, "Come to Me all you who labor and are heavy laden..." as He was speaking to the Jewish people who were suffering under a heavy load of burdensome rules put on them by the religious leaders of the day. The Pharisees, the religious leaders of the day, had a rule problem. They were experts in law keeping, but it seemed the laws they expected others to obey they might not have been keeping themselves. This is what Jesus had to say:

> Jesus said to the crowds and to his disciples: The Pharisees and the teachers of the Law are experts in the Law of Moses. So obey everything they teach you, but don't do as they do. After all, they say one thing and do something else. They pile heavy burdens on people's shoulders and won't lift a finger to help. Everything they do is just to show off in front of others. They even make a big show of wearing Scripture verses on their foreheads and arms, and they wear big tassels for everyone to see. They love the best seats at banquets and the front seats in the meeting places. And when they are in the market, they like to have people greet them as their teachers.
>
> Matthew 23:1-7 (CEV)

What a tragedy to be told to obey everything they teach you but not to do as they do. He went on to call them hypocrites for speaking one thing and doing another. He also called them blind guides who were like whitewashed tombs. It seems rather harsh, doesn't it? After all, these were the priests, the spiritual leaders, but Jesus knew that they were in it for the wrong reasons. They liked the power, the fame, and the money that their position brought them. Rather than drawing people to God, Jesus saw that they were causing people to be bound by religious rules; they were the hypocrisy within the church. So many times have I heard someone tell me that the reason they don't go to church is because of the hypocrisy within it. Many people are crushed by the failures of leaders within the church when a secret sin is brought to light. It brings great disillusionment to a place that was supposed to be safe and secure. After all, this is the church, the one place you thought you could trust people. I know people who have walked away from Jesus because they saw a spiritual leader within the church say one thing and yet do another. That's when Jesus came on the scene and said, "Hey, hook up to me! Don't do what they are doing." He wanted the people to know that the law was to be followed, but they could yoke with Him and find that with Him the law would be refreshing, not oppressing. There are still churches today that follow the traditions of men and leave Jesus out. When you have man-made rules without the relationship of Jesus you will have rebellion. I once heard Andy Stanley say; "Rules without relationship lead to rebellion."

We now live in a society rebelling against God because they see Him through the eyes of man-made rules that have missed the relationship aspect that God intended for their faith to be built on. God said, "These people honors Me with their lips, but their heart is far from Me. And in vain they worship Me, teaching as doctrines the commandments of men" (Isaiah 29:13), in the Old Testament, and Jesus repeated it to the Pharisees of His time. Would He have the same thing to say to us today? I'm afraid He might. How many go to church on a Sunday morning simply to check off the box because it is just the thing to do? How many sheep are still looking for a Shepherd to lead them?

That's exactly what Jesus saw when He walked into the lives of the multitudes around Him. When Jesus looked at them, He saw sheep without a Shepherd, and I ask myself, "Why?" They had spiritual leaders, did they not? They had the Law of Moses as a standard for life. Why were they so lost? What were they missing that the Law could not fulfill? Romans 8:2-4 gives us insight.

> The Holy Spirit will give you life that comes from Christ Jesus and will set you free from sin and death. The Law of Moses cannot do this, because our selfish desires make the Law weak. But God set you free when He sent His own Son to be like us sinners and to be a sacrifice for our sin. God used Christ's body to condemn sin. He did this, so that we would do what the Law commands by obeying the Spirit instead of our own desires.
>
> Romans 8:2-4 (CEV)

They were just going through the motions, working to obey the Law without any passion or love for it; it was only out of obligation—just a duty and a ritual they had to follow in obedience to the Jewish leaders and customs. Do you suppose there are those today doing the same thing? Are there churches today imposing legalistic rules for men to follow, leaving the joy of the relationship out? Are there churches based upon the traditions of men rather than the commands of God? I suppose there are. Look at what Jesus had this to say to the Pharisees about tradition in Matthew 15:1-3,

> Then some Pharisees and teachers of the law came to Jesus from Jerusalem and asked, "Why do your disciples break the tradition of the elders? They don't wash their hands before they eat!" Jesus replied, "And why do you break the command of God for the sake of your tradition?

Matthew 5:1-3 (NIV)

Are there times when we break the commands of God for the sake of our traditions within the church? What about the "we've always done it this way" mindset that takes on a life of its own within the church?

The Jewish people had the Messianic prophecies to look to in expectation of Jesus's arrival, yet they did not recognize Him for Who He was when He walked among them. John 1:10 tells us that, "He was in the world, and the world was made through Him, and the world did not know Him. He came to His own, and His own did not receive Him" (NKJV). Do we suffer the same blindness within our own churches at times today? We have the Word of God, the Book of Life, which reveals the truth of God's gift of grace, yet are we so stuck on our traditions that we don't recognize Him moving among us? Colossians 2:8 gives us this warning about tradition of men. "Beware lest anyone cheat you through philosophy and empty deceit, according to the tradition of men, according to the basic principles of the world, and not according to Christ" (Colossians 2:8 NKJV).

John 1:17 says, "For the law was given through Moses, but grace and truth came through Jesus Christ." Jesus didn't intend to abolish the law; He was the *fulfillment* of the Law. He said in Matthew 5:17, "Do not think that I came to destroy the Law or the Prophets. I did not come to destroy but to fulfill." We must understand that while the Law has value for us and we don't disregard it, we won't find our salvation in the Law. We can only find our salvation in Jesus and He is calling out, "Come to me all who labor…and I will give you rest." God wants you to rest from religious works and all of your legalistic rules. And to make it possible He offered His yoke.

When you put a yoke on oxen you are taking two stubborn animals and binding them together. They are now a hard-working team, walking side by side, no longer going in separate directions.

Where one goes, the other goes. This is the yoke that Jesus wants us to put on—a yoke that binds us with Him, so where He leads we will walk right along beside Him, obediently accepting His will above our own, not stubbornly fighting to be separate from the yoke pulling to go in the opposite direction. It reminds me of marriage. When I married my husband we became yoked together. We became one, and in order for our marriage to be a successful one we must go in the same direction. We shopped for and decided on what home we wanted to purchase. We were yoked in how we raised our children and how we spent our money. We make decisions based on how that decision will affect the other one. A marriage that has two people living separate lives, each fighting to do their own thing, will not be a marriage for long—at least not an intimate one. For anyone who believes that this life is only about you and you don't need to answer to anyone, this may seem like a hard pill to swallow. But putting on Christ's yoke actually brings freedom and rest.

Jesus says that His yoke is easy and His burden is light. How is it easy? Evangelist and theologian Charles Finney explains it this way:

> His yoke is easy because he never prohibits anything, and never imposes upon us any restraint except for our own good, or for the good of the race to which we belong. If at any time he restrains us, or deprives us of anything that we would like, it is love's restraint. He sees that it would be injurious to us, injurious to the world, and consequently dishonorable to him; and therefore enlightened love compels him to restrain us.
>
> Finney (1999, 2000)

"Love's restraint withholds anything that would be injurious *to us, the world* or *dishonorable to His name*." If He is putting a yoke upon us that withholds nothing except that which will cause harm to us, the world or His name, why do we fight against the yoke? If we were to "…love the Lord our God with all our heart, with all our soul, with all our mind, and with all our strength" (Mark 12:30), I believe it would be easier to wear the yoke. But for many we have lost the love and honor Him with lips only, having hearts that are far from Him. Oh, we may do "good works," believing that if we work hard enough and are good enough then, well, that should be enough. What then do we do with this verse from Ephesians? "For by grace you have been saved through faith, and that not of yourselves; it is the gift of God, not of works, lest anyone should boast" (Ephesians 2:8-9). There are many people today living out a faith based on works and because of the "law" are tied to heavy yokes of bondage. Charles Finney goes on to say,

> Let it be understood, then, that they who make religion a hard, up hill matter, have no Gospel religion. They are wearing, not Christ's yoke, but the yoke of the law; and that, too, laid upon their stiff-neckedness and unbrokenness of heart.

Taking off the yoke of religious works and putting on the yoke of Jesus is much more appealing, I think. While putting on the yoke of Jesus does still require action, it's an action based upon love. Sometimes we can become so busy worshipping our *works* within the church that we forget who we are really there to worship. We can have our list of rules and regulations, our legalistic laws, set before us and do all we can to not break any and never even meet the Son whom we are legalistically serving. How tragic.

You can be sure that when a Christian, whether a leader or not, falls, they have walked away from the yoke of Christ. When we unyoke from Him you can be certain that the effects of it will not only be upon us but everyone who is watching, as well. As a member of Christ's family it is extremely painful for me to watch another family member lose sight of Christ's yoke. It hurts me when I hear people speak against God because of those who have refused to follow loves' restraint and have allowed themselves and God to be dishonored. Hypocrisy brings injury to the family name. When you allow Him to place His yoke upon you and you sense the freedom, you will love to serve Christ. You will never want to do anything that would cause harm to Him or His name. You will find such joy in living a surrendered life to Christ you can't help but want to dance in worship, lift your hands in praise and thank Him for the remainder of your days!

So I ask you, have you allowed Christ to place His yoke upon you? Are you yoked to Him? Are you weary and worn out on religion, or have you found the joy in a full relationship? If you are weary, He is calling to you, "Come to Me. I want to give you rest." What are you waiting for?

Questions to consider:

1) What is the difference between religion and relationship?

2) Have you experienced just one or the other or both?

3) Charles Finney made the statement, "To take Christ's yoke is to commit ourselves to universal obedience to Christ from love to him, sympathy with him, and confidence in him. This is no doubt the true idea of taking Christ's yoke upon us." What does this mean to you? Please take some time and read the book of Galatians this week.

4) Read Galatians 2:16. What are we not justified by? But we are justified by what?

5) Read Galatians 3:2-3. What do you suppose Paul was asking?

6) In Galatians 3:10-14, what shall the *just* live by? What did Christ redeem us from?

7) Does our freedom from the law mean that we can live however we desire?

8) Read Galatians 5. What do you learn from this passage of scripture about grace, love, and walking in the Spirit?

9) Do you attempt to live by the law of legalism, or are you motivated by love?

10) Read Romans 7:1-6. What does verse four reveal to us? Who are we to bear fruit to? What does verse 5 tell us? And verse 6 tells us we are to serve how?

# Z IS FOR ZEALOUS

## God Says I am *Zealous* for Him

"As many as I love, I rebuke and chasten. Therefore be *zealous* and repent."

Revelation 3:19 (NKJV)

*Zealous:* full of, characterized by, or due to zeal; ardently active, devoted, or diligent (dictionary.com, 2011).

Most nights while watching the news we can hear a story about an individual or an organization, which is zealous for a cause in which they believe. Some we may agree with, some we may not. There have been times when I have understood the passion and reasoning while there have been other times when it has made no sense at all to me. But when I think back to nearly twenty years ago when the Lord opened my spiritual eyes to Him, I know that there were those who understood my passion while there were those to whom it made no sense at all. I was very zealous, to say the least. I had so much passion and excitement for the Lord that I thought everyone should feel and believe the same way I was. It made for some pretty miserable days in my life because not everyone wanted to hear what I had to share. Not everyone wanted to do what I thought they should do, and most importantly, not everyone was going to believe how

I thought they should believe. I have a tendency to get really excited over the things of God. When I have a sense that God, is moving or I recognize that I have heard Him speaking, I can get *really* excited. And sometimes in my excitement I can become very zealous. I like the dictionary definition: ardently active. It is being "intensely devoted." That's me when I sense God's speaking to my heart—"ardently active" or intensely devoted and passionate—and not only can it be hard to keep up with me, but it might be hard to *understand* me. I have had to learn to be very careful in my zeal because sometimes I have said and done things that have had more of a negative affect rather than a positive one. I believe that can be true for any of us and it is important for us to be watchful over.

We have all heard the stories about people or groups of Christians who commit crimes of murder or violence toward those they view are in opposition to God and the Word. We have been witnesses to abortion doctors being gunned down, clinics blown up, and threats made against them. News coverage can be found about Christian militia groups preparing to do battle against the government. We can find websites full of reasons why God hates America and why we are going to hell. Interesting viewpoints and interpretations of the Bible can be easily found these days. Different from mine, but we do have something in common; they, like me, are very zealous for what they believe. And like me, at times they might have more of a negative affect on people rather than a positive one. We hold our beliefs based upon the Bible, and we use scripture to support our convictions, but I cannot help but wonder if this verse found in Proverbs, "Do not let your heart envy sinners, but be zealous for the fear of the Lord all the day" (Proverbs 23:17), isn't a verse that we should embrace a little more tightly. It is very important to be zealous for the Lord, God indeed wants us to be zealous for Him, but we can discover that our zeal really needs to be *for* the fear of the Lord, and that is a good thing. If we were to have the proper fear of the

Lord in our zeal for Him there would be a protection for us that would help prevent us from misunderstanding and wrongfully interpreting the scriptures. Too many people these days are taking scriptures out of context to make it say what they want to hear rather than what they need to hear. Paul told Timothy in 2 Timothy 4:3 that this would happen. He wrote to him, "For the time will come when men will not put up with sound doctrine. Instead, to suit their own desires, they will gather around them a great number of teachers to say what their itching ears want to hear" (NIV).

Oh, we must be so careful to interpret the Word of God as it was intended and not misuse God's Word by taking scriptures out of the context in which they were written. We are led astray when we try to take the Word and change it fit to our desires rather than allowing the truth of the Word change us to fit it. God never intended for us to make His Word comfortable for us to hear. We must be challenged by it; it should convict us to change! Our pastors and teachers are not doing their job if they are not teaching us the Word in truth and without apology. I once heard a Pastor say over and over during one of his messages, "I'm sorry if I might be stepping on your toes with this message." I wanted to stand up and shout, "You are, and it hurts, but that is exactly what you are called to do! Stop apologizing for it!"

When Peter wrote the book of 2 Peter, this was his greeting:

May grace (God's favor) and peace (which is perfect well-being, all necessary good, all spiritual prosperity, and freedom from fears and agitating passions and moral conflicts) be multiplied to you in [the full, personal, precise, and correct] knowledge of God and of Jesus our Lord.

2 Peter 1:2 (Amplified Bible)

KOLLEEN LUCARIELLO

The original Greek translation is for "precise and correct knowledge." That is exactly what Peter wanted for those who read his writings—correct knowledge of God and of Jesus. He wanted people to know them and understand everything about them correctly. If I wrote a letter to one of my kids with instructions for them to carry out, I would want them to interpret the letter as I intended it, not twist my words and decide they were going to interpret it however they saw fit. If there were an area of concern or a lack of understanding, I would want them to seek out true understanding. If there was something they couldn't quite figure out I would want them to look at my character, who I am, and all I stand for to determine what I meant. If it made them a little uncomfortable while reading it, I would hope they would understand I had their best interest in mind when I wrote it. We must be precise and correct in our knowledge of the Word and in our understanding. We do not want to become so heavenly minded that we aren't any earthly good, but we also do not want to be complacent in our faith. Now you may ask, "Aren't we supposed to change? Aren't we supposed to be zealous for the Lord?" Absolutely, but a lesson I learned along the way was the importance of balance. We must be careful to remain balanced in every area of our lives even in our walk with the Lord.

In Luke 2:52 we are told that as Jesus grew He "…increased in wisdom and stature, and in favor with God and men." The key areas in our lives where balance must be found are found in this verse: physical, mental, social, and spiritual. If one of these areas is lacking our attention, we are out of balance. First Peter 5:8 from the Amplified Bible tells us to, "Be well balanced (temperate, sober of mind), be vigilant and cautious at all times; for that enemy of yours, the devil, roams around like a lion roaring [in fierce hunger], seeking someone to seize upon and devour."

While we must remember that we have authority over the enemy and his schemes, it is up to us to make sure that we are well balanced in our lives. Balance is a massive area in our lives

226

where I see Satan really likes to play around. If he can get us off balance in one area then he knows we will be off in other areas, as well, especially in our walk with the Lord. For example, he knows that if he is able to get us out of balance in our work and we become a workaholic then our relationship with our family will suffer. Relationships break down when too much of our time is spent elsewhere. If he can get us off balance in our eating and exercise then he knows our health will suffer. And if he knows he can get us off balance in our thinking and understanding of the Word of God, then our witness to the world will suffer. As we live in a time where terrorist attacks take place, quite often, we comment and wonder how people can think that such violence is ever of God. Proverbs 27:7 gives us a little hint in understanding how people can get caught up in cults and deception. It says, "He who is full loathes honey, but to the hungry even what is bitter tastes sweet" (NIV). When people are hungry, anything tastes good, and people are hungry today—spiritually hungry. We may not recognize our hunger as spiritual, but the Lord has shown me in my own life that when I am out of balance it is often because I have allowed my devotional time with Him to slip. When Satan schemes to get people out of balance in the Word and off of God's course for their lives, there may be a lot of zeal, but is it correctly placed?

The word *zealous* from Revelation 3:19 comes from the Greek word *zēloō,* and one of the definitions is "to be zealous in the pursuit of good" (Blue Letter Bible, 1996-2011). While being zealous for God and wanting to defend and uphold to Him and His teachings is right, God desires for us to be balanced in living our lives in such a way that it draws men to Him, not turns them off to Him. How we behave determines how people are going to view God. When I discovered that being zealous for the Lord also meant being zealous in the pursuit of good…wow. What an eye-opener that was! Jesus said in Matthew 12, "For out of the abundance of the heart the mouth speaks. A good man out of the good treasure of his heart brings forth good things, and an evil man out of the evil treasure brings forth evil things" (Matthew 12:34-35). The good treasure within me is the Word of God, and it brings forth good things. I can be zealous in the pursuit of good by allowing the Word of God to dwell within me and use it as a guide in my life to help me live a well-balanced life, a life that brings honor and glory to Him. People are watching God's children, and when they see us, do they see a God of love and compassion or a God that is demanding and harsh? Do they hear love and devotion when you speak of Him, or do they hear rules and condemnation? We can be balanced in our speech. We can allow the words of Christ to dwell within us and speak them out when it is appropriate. Colossians 3:16 says to:

> Let the word [spoken by] Christ (the Messiah) have its home [in your hearts and minds] and dwell in you in [all its] richness, as you teach and admonish and train one another in all insight and intelligence and wisdom [in spiritual things, and as you sing] psalms and hymns and spiritual songs, making melody to God with [His] grace in your hearts.
>
> Colossians 3:16 (Amplified Bible)

It amazes me how easy it is for us to allow ourselves to speak the unkind words about someone, words that tear someone down rather than the words that build one another up. While baking cookies the other day with my daycare children, one little boy began wiping the flour from his hand onto the shirt of another. When I asked him what he was doing he said, "I am wiping the dirtiness off me." When I suggested that he stop, he replied, "Well, I don't want it on *me*!" I pondered that statement. Jesus said that if we don't have a good treasure within our hearts then evil is brought forth. Don't we wipe our dirtiness off on others when we allow the evil that is within our hearts to pour out upon others? We don't want it on us, so we allow it to come out in our treatment of those around us. If we had the "good treasure" of the Word dwelling richly within us and zealously pursued good, our treatment of others might look a little different. We might not be so quick to send that text message of hateful words. We might think twice before posting our grievances or rants on our social network site. We just might find that we are able to overlook offences or forgive a little quicker. Wouldn't that shake a world up for Jesus?

When the Lord presents an opportunity for you to share what He has done for you, share it with humility and in love. Let the love in our hearts and the thankfulness we feel for Christ be shared with zealousness but also reverently and with proper fear and respect of the Lord. There are those who might go to the extreme in their commitment to Christ, and then there are others who live at the other end of the spectrum, those who attend church but never really surrender to Him. We have to be careful that we aren't so worried about what others think that we don't share anything about Christ when He presents an opportunity for us. We should love Him more than anything and desire to share all we can about Him, but be careful we do not become lazy or complacent, either. Remember, Christ had this against the Ephesus Church, "But I have this [one charge to make] against you: that you have left (abandoned) the love that you had at first [you have deserted Me, your first love]" (Revelation 2:4, Amplified Bible).

If we are to reach out to people with the hope of Jesus Christ then we must believe in the Hope of Jesus Christ. If we are going to reach people with the love of Jesus Christ then we must believe in the Love of Jesus Christ. We can't give to others what we really don't have in ourselves. Let's commit ourselves to becoming students of God's Word—students who are taught correctly by those who know how to "rightly divide" scripture or "handle it accurately." Zeal comes out of our love for Christ and all that He has provided for us. Let's be careful to remain well-balanced in all areas of our lives but especially in our walk with the Lord and in our understanding of His Word. Let's live our lives zealously pursuing good so others can see Him in us. It is a wonderful thing to be zealous for the Lord and all He has provided for us. I want to live the rest of my days knowing that I have a *proper* zeal for the Lord and that my knowledge of Him is correct, and because of that others want to know more about Him. How do you want to live the rest of your days? "Behold, I stand at the door and knock. If anyone hears My voice and opens the door, I will come in to him and dine with him, and he with Me" (Revelation 3:20).

Questions to consider:

1) How would you describe a zealous person? Are you one?

2) How do people get off track in their zeal for God? Are there other areas where we can see this happen?

3) Of the four areas in our lives—mental, physical, spiritual, social—which one would you say is the most balanced in your life? Which is the least balanced?

4) What is lacking from each of these areas in your life, and what can you do to make sure all areas are equally balanced? How can we prevent ourselves from getting out of balance?

5) What can we learn from Proverbs 30:5-6?

6) Agur asked God to do what in Proverbs 30:7-8? What does verse 9 say the reason was for asking this? What can we learn from this?

7) What does David ask the Lord to do in Psalm 141:3-4?

8) What do we learn from Psalm 14:2-3? What is God looking for?

9) List the five actions David says he will do in Psalm 101:1-3.

10) How can we zealously pursue good?

# AFTERWORD

Thank you for taking this journey with me. I pray that you are able to see yourself differently than when you began. Can you? Is it possible for you to allow God to change your view on how He sees you? With His help, you can! I know that for certain. Maybe you have not yet discovered the freedom that a relationship with Christ can bring you. Do you know that He died to bring you life? Real life. Eternal life. If you have never asked Jesus to be your Savior, I invite you to do so. In 1 John 1:9 it says that "if we confess our sins, He is faithful and just to forgive us our sins and to cleanse us from all unrighteousness." Confess your sins to Him. Tell Him you are a sinner and ask Him to cleanse you. Get into a church that teaches the true Word of God and don't be afraid to change. Don't be afraid to let go of the old and welcome the new! A beautiful life is waiting for you. May the Lord's richest blessings be yours!

# CONTACT

Contact Kolleen and find out more, at

Website: www.speakkolleen.com
email: speakkolleen@gmail.com
Facebook: facebook.com/speakkolleen

# BIBLIOGRAPHY

(2011). Retrieved 10 30, 2011, from dictionary.com: http://dictionary.reference.com/browse/desire

Alexander, D. a. (Ed.). (1992). *Eerdmans Handbook to the Bible.* Oxford, England: Lion Publishing/ Wm. B. Eerdmans Publishing Co.

Berenstain, S. &. (1983). *The Berenstain Bears and The Truth.* New York, New York, USA: Random House. Inc.

*Blue Letter Bible.* (1996-2011). Retrieved 12 3, 2011, from Blueletterbible.org: http://www/blueletterbible.org/lang/lexicon/lexicon.cfm?Strongs=H3374&t=KJV

*Blue Letter Bible.* (1996-2011). Retrieved 12 4, 2011, from Blue Letter Bible: http://www.blueletterbible.org/lang/lexicon/lexicon.cfm?Strongs=G1228&t-KJV

*Blue Letter Bible.* (1996-2011). Retrieved 12 17, 2011, from Blueletterbible.org: http://www.blueletterbible.org/lang/lexicon/lexicon.cfm?Strongs=G2206&t=KJV

Dictionary, W. E. (2011). *dictionary.com.* Retrieved 11 1, 2011, from dictionary.com: http://dictionary.reference.com/browse/establish

*dictionary.com.* (2011). Retrieved 10 30, 2011, from dictionary.com: http://dictionary.reference.com/browse/change

*dictionary.com.* (2011). Retrieved 10 30, 2011, from dictionary.com: http://dictionary.reference.com/browse/accepted

dictionary.com. (2011). Retrieved 11 1, 2011, from http://dictionary.reference.com/browse/forgive

*dictionary.com.* (2011). Retrieved 11 1, 2011, from dictionary.com: http://dictionary.reference.com/browse/father

*dictionary.com.* (2011). Retrieved 11 1, 2011, from dictionary. com: http://dictionary.reference.com/browse/holy
*dictionary.com.* (2011). Retrieved 10 30, 2011, from dictionary. com: http://dictionary.reference.com/browse/image
*dictionary.com.* (2011). Retrieved 11 1, 2011, from dictionary. com: http://dictionary.reference.com/browse/justified
*dictionary.com.* (2011). Retrieved 10 30, 2011, from dictionary. com: http://dictionary.reference.com/browse/absolve
*dictionary.com.* (2011). Retrieved 10 30, 2011, from dictionary. com: http://dictionary.reference.com/browse/known
*dictionary.com.* (2011). Retrieved 10 30, 2011, from dictionary. com: http://dictionary.reference.com/browse/loved
*dictionary.com.* (2011). Retrieved 10 30, 2011, from dictionary. com: http://dictionary.reference.com/browse/mind
*dictionary.com.* (2011). Retrieved 11 8, 2011, from dictionary. com: http://dictionary.reference.com/browse/new
*dictionary.com.* (2011). Retrieved 11 18, 2011, from dictionary. com: http://dictionary.reference.com/browse/beat
*dictionary.com.* (2011). Retrieved 11 19, 2011, from dictionary. com: http://dictionary.reference.com/browse/qualified
*dictionary.com.* (2011). Retrieved 11 19, 2011, from dictionary. com: http://dictionary.reference.com/browse/righteous
*dictionary.com.* (2011, 10 19). Retrieved 10 19, 2011, from dictionary.com, LLC: http://dictionary.reference.com/browse/secure
*dictionary.com.* (2011). Retrieved 12 2, 2011, from dictionary. com,LLC: http://dictionary.reference.com/browse/wise
*dictionary.com.* (2011). Retrieved 12 2, 2011, from dictionary.com, LLC: http://dictionary.reference.com/browse/wisdom
*dictionary.com.* (2011). Retrieved 12 3, 2011, from dictionary.com, LLC: http://dictionary.reference.com/browse/exclude
*dictionary.com.* (2011). Retrieved 12 3, 2011, from dictionary. com, LLC: http://dictionary.reference.com/browse/blessed

*dictionary.com.* (2011). Retrieved 12 4, 2011, from dictionary. com, LLC: http://dictionary.reference.com/browse/yoke

*dictionary.com.* (2011). Retrieved 12 18, 2011, from dictionary. com LLC: http://dictionary.reference.com/browse/zealous

dictionary.com. (2011, October 15). *dictionary.com.* Retrieved 2011, from dictionary.com: http://dictionary.reference. com/browse/endued

dictionary.com. (2011, 10). *dictionary.com, LLC.* Retrieved 10 30, 2011, from dictionary.com: http://dictionary.reference. come/browse/beauty

*dictionary.com, LLC.* (2011). Retrieved 10 22, 2011, from dictionary.com: http://dictionary.reference.com/browse/ treasure

*dictionary.com, LLC.* (2011). Retrieved 10 22, 2011, from dictionary.com: http://dictionary.com.reference.com/ browse/understand

*dictionary.com, LLC.* (2011). Retrieved 11 19, 2011, from dictionary.com: http://dictionary.reference.com/browse/ victorious

Dove. (2011). *Dove Campaign for Real Beauty.* (Unilever, Producer) Retrieved 10 30, 2011, from Dove: http://www. dove.us/Social-Mission/campaign-for-real-beauty.aspx

Finney, C. G. (1999,2000). *The Gospel Truth.* Retrieved 12 6, 2011, from Christ's Yoke is Easy: http://www.gospeltruth. net/18610102_christs_yoke.htm

Grall, T. S. (2009). *United States Census Department.* Retrieved 10 22, 2011, from Custodial Mothers and Fathers and Their Child Support: http://www/census.gov/prod/2009pubs/ p60-237.pdf

*Joniearecksontadastory.com.* (n.d.). Retrieved from Joni Eareckson Tada Story: http://joniearecksontadastory.com/ jonis-story-page-2

Katersky, A. (2011, October 5). *ABC News, the Blotter.* Retrieved 10 22, 2011, from abcNews The Blotter: http://abcnews.

go.com/Blotter/bernie-madoff-victims-money-back/
story?id=14672278

Moore, B. (2001). *To Live is Christ.* Nashville, TN: B & H Publishing Group.

Moore, B. (2001). *To Live is Christ.* B&H Publishing Group.

*Nelson's* NKJV *Study Bible.* (1997). Thomas Nelson, Inc.

Schoenstadt, M. A. (2009, February 09). *eMEDTV.* Retrieved 10 22, 2011, from eMEDTV Health Information Brought to Life: http://depression.emedtv.com/depression-in-woman.html

Scriven, J. M.-1. (n.d.). *Cyberhymnal.com.* Retrieved 10 22, 2011, from http://www.cyberhymnal.org/htm/w/a/f/wafwhij.htm

Simmons, A. (1999-2011). *How Does a Caterpillar Turn into a Butterfly?* Retrieved 11 18, 2011, from eHow.com: http://www.ehow.com/how-does_4563960_caterpillar-turn-butterfly.html

Strongs. (1996-2011). *Blue Letter Bible.* Retrieved 11 1, 2011, from blueletterbible.org: http://blueletterbible.org/lang/lexicon/lexicon.cfm?Strongs+H3559&t_KJV

Strong's. (1996-2011). *Blue Letter Bible.* Retrieved September 19, 2011, from Blue Letter Bible: http://www.blueletterbible.org/lang/lexicon/lexicon.cfm?Strongs=G3053&t=KJV

Strongs. (1996-2011). *Blue Letter Bible.* Retrieved September 19, 2011, from Blueletterbible.org: http://www.blueletterbible.org/lang/lexicon/lexicon.cfm?Strongs=G4995&t-KJV

Strongs. (1996-2011). *Blue Letter Bible- Lexicon.* Retrieved September 21, 2011, from Blue Letter Bible: http://www.blueletterbible.org/lexicon.cfm?Strongs=G352&&t=KJV

Strongs. (1996-2011). *Blueletterbible.org.* Retrieved 10 30, 2011, from Blue Letter Bible: http://www.blueletterbible.org/lang/lexicon/lexicon.cfm?Strongs=G1344&t=KJV

Strong's. H2713.

Suess, D. (1975). *Oh the Thinks You Can Think.* Random House, Inc.

The Handbook of Bible Application. *The Handbook of Bible Application.* (N. S. Wilson, Ed.) Wheaton, Illonois: Tyndale House Publishers.

Warren, R. (2002). *The Purpose Driven Life.* Grand Rapids, MI: Zondervan.

*Who's Who in the Bible.* (1994). Pleasantville, NY: The Reader's Digest Association.